ART AND HI

CHÂTEAUX AND CITIES
OF THE LOIRE

BONECHI

Project and editorial conception:
Casa Editrice Bonechi
Publication Manager: Giovanna Magi
Picture research: Giovanna Magi,
Monica Bonechi
Graphics: Sonia Gottardo
Video layout: Elena Nannucci
Cover: Sonia Gottardo
Editing: Patrizia Fabbri
Drawings and map: Stefano Benini
The coat of arms of the Loire was prepared by
Roberto Ciabani

Contributors:
François Bonneau, Henri de Linarès,
Simone D'Huart, Monique Jacob,
François Lemaire, Daniel Oster, Jean Saint-Bris,
Martine Tissier de Mallerais, Patrizia Fabbri,
Maurizio Martinelli, Giuliano Valdes

© Copyright by Casa Editrice Bonechi,
via Cairoli 18/b Florence - Italy
E-mail:bonechi@bonechi.it

Diffusion: OVET-PARIS
13, rue des Nanettes-75011 Paris
Tel. 43 38 56 80

Printed in Italy by
Centro Stampa Editoriale Bonechi.

The photographs are the property of the
Casa Editrice Bonechi Archives and were taken by:
Gianni Dagli Orti, Paolo Giambone,
Andrea Pistolesi.

Photo page 14: The Art Archive /
Musée du Louvre Paris / Dagli Orti (A).

Photo page 18 above: a courtesy of the
Château of Meung-sur-Loire.
Photo page 62 above: a courtesy of the
Château of Valençay.
Photos pages 84, 85 below, 88, 89, 90, 91:
a courtesy of the Château of Chenonceau.
Photo page 100 below: a courtesy of the
Château of Amboise.
Photo page 131: a courtesy of the
Château of Ussé.
Photos page 138: a courtesy of the
Château of Montsoreau.
Photo page 139 below: a courtesy of the
Château of Montreuil-Bellay.
Photos page 142, the four photos above:
A. Laurioux/ENE, Casa Editrice Bonechi Archives.

The publisher will be grateful for information
concerning the sources of photographs
without credits and will be pleased to
acknowledge them in future editions.

ISBN 88-476-1862-2
www.bonechi.com

* * *

Amboise

Blois

Chambord

Chenonceau

Contents

INTRODUCTION

*I*t seems natural to wonder why so many châteaux are situated along a river and its tributaries on a patch of land 200 kilometres long and 100 wide. The single most valid reason is that when the members of the house of Valois returned from the wars in Italy (begun in 1494) their ideas of "residence" and "court" were no longer the same. Their castles, which up to then had been little more than rude strongholds, had lost their raison d'être, for peace at home was now ensured and the invention of artillery had turned walls that seemed impregnable into fragile screens. Charles VIII, Louis XII and Francis I had assimilated the Italian model in which the measure of royal power was no longer armed might but culture, elegance, ostentation, a daily life immersed in luxury and a love of the spectacular and of show. Louis XII had called Laurana and Niccolò Spinelli from Italy and had left the palace of the Louvre for Plessis-lès-Tours. This is how it all began. Italian culture had made an impact. When Charles VIII returned from Naples in 1495, Italian artists followed in his wake. The old strongholds began to be opened up, the walls were removed and light was finally allowed to enter. Only a few characteristic elements of the castle-fortress still remained: the machicolations, for example, were transformed into ornamental motifs (Amboise, Chaumont, Chenonceau, Azay-le-Rideau, Chambord). Openings were surrounded by friezes, and chimneys made their appearance on the roofs as real sculptural elements.

Landscape gardening, with its fountains, ornamental waterworks and hedges alternated with flowerbeds, developed into an art together with the art of living. Among the artists who accompanied Charles VIII when he returned from Italy was Fra' Pacello da Marcogliano, the inventor of landscaping, who had ponce resided at the court of Naples and had never forgotten the precise green geometrical patterns of the Sicilian orange groves. When he was in Naples, Charles VIII had lived in Poggioreale which was more like a stage set for fêtes and periods of relaxation than a castle. When he returned to France, he transformed the old fortress of Amboise into a series of halls, gardens, terraces, galleries. Charles d'Amboise,

sent to Milan by order of his king, Louis XII, returned overcome by the splendid life at court and the pomp and ceremony of the Visconti court and he, too, transformed his castle of Meillant. This was when the Loire acquired a central role in the arts. The flamboyant style of the châteaux is a new dimension in the art of the court. The nobility and the new wealth of the bourgeoisie gravitated around the court. Bankers and financiers such as Berthelot at Azay-le-Rideau, Bohier at Chenonceau, were so powerful that the kings graciously accepted loans from them. And there were also merchants like Jacques Coeur, whose ships and storehouses overflowing with silks, cotton, spices and products of the Orient can still

be admired today in the stained glass windows in Bourges. And there was also Salviati, the Italian banker, whose chief merit in addition to making loans to nobles and kings is that of having had a daughter, Cassandra, who served as inspiration for Ronsard, the greatest Renaissance poet in French literature. Peace at home and the absence of tensions along the borders permitted the kings to carry on a policy of prestige and splendour which was externalized in the lacy pile of stone which is Chambord, and which, like Versailles later on, was intended to dazzle Europe. Even the ambassador of the Serenissima was left breathless – and he came from Venice. And the nobles sought to emulate the life style of the king. The Amboise family built Chaumont; the house of Hurault, Cheverny. The cities began to be built in the style which still survives in their historical centres: Tours, Blois, Angers, Orléans, cities that seem to have been carved, not constructed. It was pure chance that on May 29, 1418, the history of the Loire as a royal residence began with the flight of the dauphin of France (the future Charles VII), who sought refuge in Bourges from the Burgundian hordes. Had they wanted to, the kings who succeeded him could have returned to live in Paris once it had been reconquered. Instead they chose to live on the banks of the river. And thus for 170 years, one of the most resplendent periods in the history of France unravelled along the valley of the Loire. The river was a vital waterway along which the square sails of the boats and barges slowly moved. It was the natural way to the sea which it meets at Nantes. Silks, spices, pearls, precious stones, works of art, war trophies all arrived via the river. Charles VIII had his Italian booty brought up the river: one hundred and thirty tapestries, 39 leather wall panels with scenes in gold, lengths of velvet and damasks, illuminated books, paintings and sculpture. The booty was accompanied by tailors, cabinet-makers, makers of organs, decorators, a maker of artificial incubators and even a parrot breeder. The river too, and a project for the canal of Amboise, is how Francis I convinced Leonardo, who was already old, to follow him to France with "La Gioconda", which he bought for 4,000 ducats. The grand old man lived in Clos-Lucé, in the residence prepared for him, in close contact with the king. Here he received frequent visits, the honour and the respect his fame inspired. Besides canals, Leonardo designed automata which frightened the court ladies, fireworks and great public illuminations which concluded the days spent hunting in Amboise and Chambord. The guests were ambassadors, important dignitaries and sovereigns. Among these was the Emperor Charles V, who considered the castle as a "summus" of human ingenuity. A glimpse of court life in the 16th century may also be useful in understanding the period. In 1539, when Charles V, emperor of Spain and Flanders, arrived in Chambord, the whole valley was in ferment. Fêtes of all kinds, perhaps the most sumptuous ever planned, were in preparation. Long rows of wagons, servants unloading enormous quantities of food: oysters and fish from the Atlantic, huge trophies of fruit, plumed wildfowl, quarters of deer, barrels of wine. Tables set with silver, roaring fires. Walls lined with fabrics, the perfume of incense, lutes, guitars, torches held by pages, with light flickering on the fresh complexions and jewels of the ladies. In the procession the king and the queen, young princesses and princes of Europe, were the dauphin Henry II and his young wife Catherine de' Medici, who learned the lesson well and later organized ceremonies that were grander and more ruinous. The fêtes, the balls, the tournaments, were the culminating moment in the life of a court that also lived on intrigue: stories of repudiated wives, of ill-assorted marriages, of murders, courtesans and secret struggles for power. All set against the backdrop of the châteaux which became more and more beautiful. Every residence, be it royal, noble, or bourgeois, has its stories and secret lives which will be discovered in the pages that follow. From the murder of the Duke of Guise to the perfidious play of jealousy between the great Catherine de' Medici and the equally powerful courtesan Diane de Poitiers, to whom Henry II had given, as a gift, one of the less spectacular but more amenable châteaux, Chenonceau, which at the death of the king returned into the hands of the queen. She installed herself in the castle with her "Escadron Volant" consisting of the youngest and loveliest ladies of France whose role was that of entertaining the palace guests. The fêtes were no longer the fabulous and regal spectacles they once had been but now were a matter of play: disguises, verdant hiding places, a switching of roles. Extravagances in which the lovely ladies of the "Escadron Volant" dressed (or undressed) as available Nymphs (as described by Brantôme) served sumptuous banquets in the shade of grottoes. Catherine's decadence and refinement was handed down and accentuated in the three kings she bore to Henry II – Francis II, Charles IX and above all Henry III, the most frivolous and immoral of all, who alternated between mystical crises and the most licentious entertainment which cost the treasury a fortune and his subjects exorbitant, crushing taxes. Then came the religious wars, the night of St Bartholomew (August 24, 1572), the plague which appeared more than once – in 1583, in 1584 and in 1586. In 1607 it decimated the population of Tours. Dearth and famine followed. The fortunes of the nobles and the upper bourgeoisie melted away in their attempts to imitate the ostentation of the court. The valley was impoverished. The important silk industries languished, agriculture was neglected. The decline of the valley coincided with the end of the house of Valois. The regal processions which wound their way through the valley from fêtes and entertainment in one dwelling to those in another continued to dwindle. Palaces that were large, and stable, and monumental began to be appreciated.

The star of Fontainebleau waxed brighter. The châteaux of the Loire had reached the end of their roles as leading actors, and they now stand as extraordinary witnesses of times gone by and gems of a glorious epoch.

Elsa Nofri Rosi

The elegant outline of the château of Gien, with its unmistakeable red brick façade, mirrored on the waters of the Loire.

GIEN

The city of Gien, situated in the valley of the Loire, which is rich in game, has always been an important centre for hunting and has even earned the name of "Capital of the Hunt". Game has always been abundant in the immense forests of Orléans (34,000 hectares) which skirt the Loire from Gien to the Beauce. Gien is the northeast gate of the Sologne and the Loire is a stopping place for migratory animals. The château of Gien was therefore an ideal location for the creation of an **International Museum of the Hunt**. The building was built in 1484 on the site of a royal hunting rendezvous by Anne de Beaujeu, eldest daughter of Louis XI and Regent of France, who had received this Crown possession from the king. It consists of a vast building with windows that open to the south, overlooking the city below and the Loire and the countryside on the horizon. To the east another building, at right angles to the first, looks out on the river which lazily winds down towards the valley and as far as the horizon where the hills of Sancerre can just barely be distinguished.

The façades on the inner courtyard, less severe in their lines, are pleasingly embellished by three small octagonal towers in brick and stone with fine stone spiral staircases inside; above are square rooms, flanked again by round turrets which enclose narrower staircases.

When Anne de Beaujeu died, the castle returned to the Crown. Within these walls in 1523 Francis I signed the docu-

ment which conferred the regency on Louise of Savoy. Henry II stayed here, as did Catherine de' Medici and Charles IX during the Religious Wars.

The château belonged in turn to various great families until the county of Gien was suppressed during the Revolution. In 1823 the château was acquired by the department of Loiret.

The collections are lively and instructive. Chronologically arranged, they tell the story of hunting throughout the centuries by means of hunter's weapons as well as drawings, etchings, paintings, tapestries, decorated ceramics and accessories.

There are flintlock guns with extremely long barrels to ensure a greater firing range and to make it possible to shoot from horseback without running the risk of hitting one's mount, as well as two-barrelled guns. These firearms, sculpted, engraved, damascened, inlaid with ivory, tortoise shell, mother-of-pearl or precious metals, are in themselves works of art. The lovely room on the first floor contains more than 75 paintings and studies by François Desportes (1661-1743). He was assigned to the person of King Louis XIV and followed him when he went hunting, painting the finest game the king had killed as well as portraits of his best dogs: Blanche, Ponne, Zette, and others. Gifted with a unique skill, he worked with an untiring virtuosity. He executed large decorations for the royal and princely houses and large hunting scenes of all kinds. It is particularly interesting to compare the projects or studies and the large finished paintings. Two large canvases by J. B. Oudry (1686-1755), who was Desportes' successor as

painter of the king's hunts, have been hung near the latter artist's paintings so that the two styles can be compared. In fact, for a long time Oudry was the better known of the two even though he seems never to have done anything of the same standard. An exception is the large "Wolf Hunt" in the Museum which, experts agree, is one of the painter's best works. In 1972 the Museum was presented with

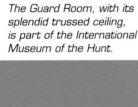

The Guard Room, with its splendid trussed ceiling, is part of the International Museum of the Hunt.

the exceptional collection of the personal trophies of Claude Hettier de Boislambert, Grand Chancellor of the Order of the Liberation and Honorary President of the International Hunting Council. Claude Hettier de Boislambert was primarily interested in protecting nature and animals. He was an exemplary hunter and conceived of hunting as rational exploitation and regulation of natural resources. The 500 trophies on exhibition were collected in the course of 50 years of hunting as a sport. The animals to be killed were always carefully chosen and always "approached" on foot. An entire room is dedicated to a rare collection of 5,000 hunting buttons, small works of art created for the tunics of the supervisors of the royal hunts. More than 50 hunting horns, set against a background of the colours of the royal hunt, trace the evolution of the horn from the time of Louis XIV to the present day.

The Guard Room contains numerous pictures and studies by François Desportes (1661-1743), the artist of the royal hunt.

BRIARE

In 1890, in order to join two canals without flowing into the Loire, work began on constructing a canal-bridge, 664 metres long, to cross the river. Opened in 1897, this veritable work of art, made of stone and metallic structures and designed with the assistance of Gustave Eiffel, receives a one way navigable waterway, regularly used by boats and flanked by two paths reserved for pedestrians and cyclists.

ST-BRISSON

The castle of Saint-Brisson is located in the village of the same name, just a few kilometres south of Gien, on the left bank of the Loire. Originally it was a military fortress that was besieged by

The many attractions of St Brisson include four reproductions of medieval war machines exhibited in the moat of the castle; operated by figures in period costume, since 1991 they have attracted many visitors.

King Louis VI; King Philippe Auguste stayed there in 1181. The castle's layout dates from the 12th century: it was a regular hexagon (part of which no longer exists) of buildings, enclosed by alternating square and round towers. The castle was considerably modified in the 17th and 19th centuries. The rooms, too, were drastically changed in the 19th and 20th centuries.

LA BUSSIÈRE

The castle is located at the far end of the village of La Bussière. In the 12th century, Etienne de Feins built a fortress on what is now the site of the castle to defend himself against the Bourbons. The property was inherited by Etienne Fromond, Minister of Justice under Charles VII and first president of the parliament under Louis XII. In 1518 it was inherited by Jean du Tillet, chancellor of the Parliament of Paris. Fifteen priests of Gien took refuge here during the wars of religion in 1567, but the besieged fortress fell, the priests were beheaded by the Huguenot troops and the castle was severely damaged. In the 17th century the

Tillet family began building a more tranquil residence (with outbuildings, a double circle of walls, and a drawbridge). Jean-Baptiste du Tillet, a member of Louis XIV's court, commissioned Le Nôtre to design the gardens, he also built the two pavilions at the gate and the monumental entrance. After the Revolution, as a national property, the castle was sold to the administrator of the Tillet estates, then to a wood merchant who then sold it to the count of Chasseval, ancestor of the current owners. The main building is made of brick and stone, with a slate roof; its entrance tower, at the centre of the building, dates from the 16th

century, though almost the entire structure was rebuilt at the beginning of the 18th century and was then restored with a heavy hand in the 19th. The attractive annexes in the courtyard date from the 17th century. Inside the chateau is a 16th-century kitchen built of brick with a vaulted ceiling, furnished in period style. Of particular interest are the 16th-century spiral staircase, a Venetian veranda (19th-century) that offers a lovely view of the pond, and the interesting **Musée de la pêche** (fishing museum) in the rooms that were refurbished in the 19th century.

Facing page, from the top, the castle of La Bussière, with the typical entrance tower; a view of the park; the 17th-century annexes on the courtyard.

The Château of Sully-sur-Loire, with its medieval style turret, appears to have been almost built on the water.

SULLY-SUR-LOIRE

At the entrance to the village of Sully-sur-Loire stands a medieval-looking castle surrounded by towers, that seems to rise out of the water.

In the 14th century Guy de la Trémoïlle, a favorite of King Charles V, built the rectangular donjon with four square towers and a gate with two smaller towers to the south. The building was designed by the king's architect Raymond du Temple. The "small castle" was built in the mid-fifteenth century: it encloses the courtyard south of the rectangular donjon, and comprises a house and two towers that herald the Renaissance. In 1602 Maximilien de Béthune, King Henry IV's famous finance minister, better known as Sully, acquired the property. He built a tower in 1605 and had the interior renovated. The castle belonged to his descendants until 1962. In the 18th century another building was added to the donjon and the "small castle"; this part was entirely rebuilt after the fire of 1918.

In addition to Guy de la Trémoïlle and Sully, the castle also hosted Joan of Arc, Charles VII, Voltaire and the Marquis de La Fayette. After the death of King Henry IV, Sully wrote his *Mémoires des sages et royales économies d'Etat de Henri le Grand*. Voltaire used the great hall of honour for performances of *Artémises*, and it was at the castle that he wrote *Henriade*.

The castle is reached on foot by crossing two bridges that provide an excellent view of the whole complex. In the courtyard there is a tower built by King Philippe Auguste, and a statue of Sully. The park, of which only an extensive area surrounded by canals remains, is evidence of the major work Sully had done in the 17th century in order to protect the castle from being flooded by the river Loire. Worthy of note inside are the magnificent 300 square metre main hall with its 7 metre ceiling, the reconstructed king's bedroom, the duke's bedroom in the Renaissance pavilion and the splendid Gothic oak ceiling (late 14th century) in the upper room of the tower, shaped like an overturned ship's hull.

Every year in the early summer, Sully-sur-Loire hosts an important International Festival of Classical Music, the first grand event in the wonderful annual season of Festivals held throughout France. For over thirty years artists of world class level have performed here in the magnificent settings provided by this elegant castle. Most of the concerts and recitals are in fact held in the fine Auditorium of the château, famous for its splendid acoustics, and in the ancient and historic Guards' Room.

St-Benoît

The abbey of St-Benoît-de-Fleury, founded to receive the remains of St Benedict, enjoyed particular fortune in the Carolingian period, under the abbot Theodulphus. The massive arcaded tower (early 11th century), built high up to avoid flooding, with its cross-shaped pillars and beautiful storiated capitals and the choir (1067-1080), that rises above the crypt, surrounded by four chapels, constitute the oldest parts of the abbey. The austere and brightly-lit nave was, in fact, rebuilt in the 13th century, and probably completed in 1218. It marks the ascendancy of the new Gothic art over the elegant and linear Romanesque structures of which the abbey of St-Benoît still offers a splendid example.

Chamerolles

The château of Chamerolles was built in 1522, according to the wishes of Lancelot du Lac, governor of Orléans. Situated on the threshold of the forest of Orléans, the château was constructed as a vast stone and brick quadrilateral, consisting of three wings marked at the corners by four towers. To the east, the large courtyard is open on the side of the access tower, flanked by four small cylindrical towers. The château is surrounded by a large park, the gardens of which have recently been returned to their former splendour and opened to the public. The entire château has been meticulously restored over a lengthy period.

From the top, the arcaded tower giving access to the abbey of St-Benoît and a view of the nave. Below, view of the eastern side of the château of Chamerolles.

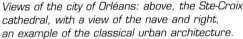
Views of the city of Orléans: above, the Ste-Croix cathedral, with a view of the nave and right, an example of the classical urban architecture.

ORLÉANS

This beautiful and interesting city, with its many historical, architectural and artistic monuments is set in a graceful position on the right bank of the Loire River. It is the capital of the Centre region and has both a busy industrial section and a flourishing rural economy based on nurseries and vineyards. It is often said that "if Paris is the head of France, Orléans is its heart". Originally called Cenabum by the Gauls, it was Romanized by Caesar's legions in 52 B.C. Under its new name of Aurelianis, it survived a siege by the Huns, and was a longtime residence of the Capetians (10-11th centuries). But the city's fame is linked to the important events that occurred during the Hundred Year's War when Joan of Arc, now the patron saint of France, freed the city from the English siege with an army provided by the dauphin, the future King Charles VII (on 8 May 1429) and earned the title of the "Maid of Orléans".

Joan of Arc

Joan of Arc (or Jehanne Darc) was born of a poor peasant family on 6 January 1412 in the village of Domrèmy in Lorraine.

It was a difficult and dramatic moment in the history of France, with a civil war raging and the feudal lords, supported by England, trying to increasingly weaken the sovereign. At the battle of Agincourt during the One Hundred Years' War (October 1415) the English archers of King Henry V defeated the proud French cavalry thus giving the English control of a large area of France and Henry was recognized as sovereign of the united kingdoms of France and England. The heir to the throne, Charles the Dauphin, and future Charles VII, was a king without a crown and without a throne, quite incapable of reversing the by now desperate situation facing France.

Joan, in the meantime, had begun hearing voices at the age of 13, "I was in the thirteenth year of my life when God sent a voice to guide me. At first I was frightened: 'I am a poor young girl who knows neither how to wage war nor how to spin' I answered. But the angel said, 'Saint Catherine and Saint Margaret will come to you. Do as they tell you for they are sent to advise and guide you and you will believe all that they tell you.'". The message was that she must free the country and save it. Firmly convinced, in February 1429, Joan contacted the head of a garrison loyal to the Dauphin, Robert de Baudricourt, and convinced him to provide her with some armed men to accompany her on a 2,500 kilometre journey through enemy-occupied territory, to Chinon to meet Charles. She was an illiterate girl of just 17 years old, yet she succeeded in convincing the Dauphin to entrust her with command of the troops sent to liberate Orléans, which was on the verge of falling after eight months of the siege laid by the army of Henry VI. Encouraged by the enthusiasm of the village folk and soldiers, with the fluttering white standard bearing the names of Jesus and Maria leading the way, Joan broke the siege and liberated the city on 8 May. From that day she would be known as the "Maid of Orléans".

With an aura of fanatical mysticism, the French army achieved further victories: at Patay, on 18 June, the English suffered losses of 10,000 men in battle and Joan succeeded in liberating the land as far as Reims, where on 17 July Charles was finally crowned king of France by archbishop Regnault, as Joan stood behind her sovereign. However, Charles then decided not to listen to the Maid, who pressed for a swift march on Paris, preferring to attempt diplomatic negotiations with the English. On her own initiative, Joan, at the head of her faithful troops, headed first for Paris where she was wounded (8 September 1429) then marching on Compiègne where she was ambushed on 24 May 1430 by the Anglo-Bourgogne troops and was captured by John of Luxembourg. Either Charles VII did not know, or he did not wish to save her and Joan was handed over to the English as a prize of war in exchange for 10,000 gold ecus. While in prison in the castle of Rouen, the trial to find her guilty of heresy and witchcraft was begun — two false accusations that were invented to deflect the political significance that her condemnation would have. Her accuser was the bishop and lord of Beauvais, Pierre Cauchon, an ally of the English. From January to May 1431, Joan refuted all accusations, opposing the judges and doctors of theology and law who sat on the ecclesiastical tribunal. Her faith and courage, however, could not, in the end, save her from death at the stake. At dawn on 30 May 1431 Joan was burnt alive in the Vieux Marché square in Rouen. As the flames enveloped her, she screamed the name of Jesus aloud six times. Two enquiries, one in 1449 and one in 1456, lead to a review of the trial and then to her complete exoneration. Beatified in 1909, she was made a saint by Pope Benedict XV on 30 May 1920, and in the same year it was decided to make her patron of France.

Jean Auguste Dominique Ingres, *Saint Joan of Arc at coronation of King Charles VII*, 1854.

The **Cathédrale Ste-Croix** is an outstanding and grandiose monument, a fine exemplary model of the French Gothic style. Although the building's origins date from the 13th century, its current appearance is the result of renovations following almost total destruction by Protestants in 1568, that began in the 17th century and lasted well into the 19th. The highly ornate façade with three grandiose portals, each surmounted by rose windows, is embellished with aedicules and crowned by an elegant loggia with ogival arches and lavish fretwork. Two graceful soaring towers (18th century) re-propose elements typical of the French Gothic style. The large statues on the façade portray the Evangelists. A steep, pointed spire rises from the transept. The vast and majestic interior has five naves. The sombre central nave is surmounted by ribbed ogival cross vaults. Amongst the most interesting features are the 18th-century woodcarvings on the choir, by Degoullons who had previously worked in Paris and at Versailles, and an early 17th-century marble statue of the Madonna carved by M. Bourdin, a local sculptor; the statue stands in the chapel located at the centre of the apse. The Chapel of Joan of Arc, to the left of the choir has a statue of Cardinal Touchet, the champion of the cult of the "Maid", who lived in the late 19th-early 20th century. The crypt contains vestiges of three ancient houses of worship that existed between the 4th and 10th centuries, and the tombs of bishops who lived between the 13th and 14th centuries where various interesting artefacts were found, now displayed in the Treasury.

Exhibited on the second floor of the **Musée des Beaux-Arts** are 15th-century works of the Sienese school, a marble statue portraying the "Virgin and Child" (14th century), and works by Italian, Flemish and Dutch artists such as Tintoretto, Correggio, Annibale Carracci, Van der Velde, Van Goyen, Pourbus, Velazquez. The paintings on the first floor are by French

Above, Place du Martroi, the real geographical centre of the town with the equestrian statue of Joan of Arc (below). Top, historic houses representing the unmistakable architecture so typical of Orléans.

masters from the 17th and 18th centuries including C. Vignon, Ph. de Champaigne, Louis le Nain, C. Deruet. Outstanding 18th-century portraitists exhibited include F. Hubert Drouais, L. Tocqué and J. B. Perronneau. Some sculptures as well as paintings by Courbet, Gauguin, Rouault, and Max Jacob complete the group of works by 19th-20th century artists.

The elegant Hôtel Cabu (16th century) is now the home of the **Musée Historique** (Historical Museum). One of its greatest masterpieces is the Gallic-Roman Treasure from Neuvy-en-Sullias. The **House of Joan of Arc** overlooking the central Place du Général de Gaulle, is the reconstruction of where the French national heroine stayed. Mementoes, audiovisual presentations and various artefacts help retell her epic story.

Other highlights at Orléans include the central, porticoed Rue Royale that leads to the panoramic **Pont George V**, the **Hôtel Groslot**, a lovely, 16th century Renaissance house, and the churches of **St-Pierre-le-Puellier** (12th century, Romanesque) and **St-Aignan** (Gothic, consecrated in 1509).

This austere but attractive château has some fascinating interiors from the elegant drawing rooms to the kitchens, as well as some famous stables.

LA FERTÉ-ST-AUBIN

La Ferté-St-Aubin stands on the banks of the Cosson, near the old part of the village where one can still admire some traditional, woodframed, brick houses of Sologne. Still inhabited after almost four centuries, this historic 3-storey residence offers visitors the opportunity to see 15 rooms perfectly furnished in period style and still in use today. Between 1590 and 1620 Henri de St-Nectaire built the existing left portion of the main building over the ruins of a castle that had been destroyed in 1562. Subsequently this was progressively enlarged by his son, Henri II de la Ferté-St-Nectaire, Marshal of France, and then by De Lowendal, also a Marshal of France, who acquired La Ferté in the mid 18th century. Access to the castle is quite spectacular from a bridge that leads to a grand monumental gate, but even more enchanting are the 17th-century **stables**. Of great historical interest, they were particularly unusual in a private castle (as they were generally the prerogative of the king) and they still function today as they did in the 19th century. Also in the stable block amidst the Spanish stallions and ponies, there is an interesting collection of *haut école* harnesses providing a unique insight into the history of the horse and equitation.

CLÉRY ST-ANDRÉ

In 1280, near Cléry, a statue of the Madonna, which soon proved to have miraculous properties, was found and placed in a chapel nearby. In its honour, Philip the Fair had a building erected which was destroyed by the English in 1428. Charles d'Orléans and his step-brother, the Count of Dunois, who entrusted the project to architects Pierre Le Paige and Pierre Chauvin, and Louis XI who, in order to fulfil a vow gave great impetus to the completion of the work, are responsible for the present Notre-Dame de Cléry. Completed in the 1400s, another three chapels were added between 1515 and 1521, another three chapels were added. One of the chapels, dedicated to St James, recalls the fact that St James of Compostela often passed through Cléry on pilgrimage. Thanks to complex restoration work, the church has reached the present day in all its splendour, having survived the devastation caused by the Huguenots in 1562 and 1567. Louis XI and his consort, Charlotte of Savoy, rest here, and their sepulchral marble monument, by Michel Bourdin (1622), dominates the left side of the nave; their son, Charles VIII was also buried, and the Count of Dunois is interred in the Longueville chapel he had built for himself and his descendants, in the middle of the 15th century, by the architect Colin du Val.

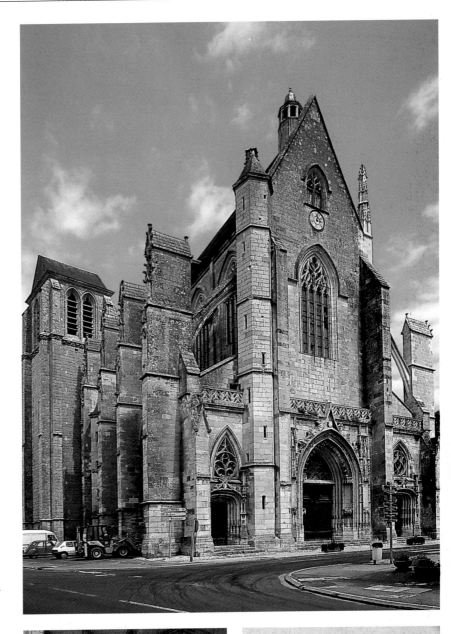

Top, the sober elegance of the façade of Notre-Dame de Cléry. Right, the funeral monument of Louis XI and Charlotte of Savoy and the tombstone of Charles VIII.

Charles VIII
1498

MEUNG-SUR-LOIRE

The castle of Meung-sur-Loire stands in the middle of the village, on a hillside on the banks of the Loire. Originally, an 11th-century medieval castle stood there that had been besieged by Louis VI the Fat, in 1101. Several generations of the Meung family lived in this castle. The last, Jehan de Meung was one of the authors of the *Roman de la Rose*. From the 12th to the 18th century the castle was the official residence of the bishops of Orléans. In the 12th century Manassès de Garlande, bishop of Orléans, ordered the building of the Manassès tower (adjacent to the collegiate church of St-Liphard). In 1361 the castle was occupied by the Anglo-Navarrese (Hugues de Calverly). In the 15th century during the Hundred Years' War, the English conquered it. On June 14, 1429, Joan of Arc attacked the city, and General Talbot fled. In the 15th century the poet François Villon was imprisoned in the dungeons. Condemned to death, he wrote his "Grand Testament" before being pardoned by King Louis XI who visited Meung. In the 17th century the castle was abandoned and fell into ruin. Subsequently, King Louis XIV offered the sum of 20,000 francs to Monsignor Fleuriau d'Armonville who initiated some important works. An annex was erected on the south side; the old towers and original building were not modified. In 1791 the castle was sold at auction to J. J. Lecoulfeux who later founded the Banque de France and became Mayor of Meung.

Views of the ancient château, with the 18th-century library and chapel of Notre-Dame, with sculpted wooden doors.

François Villon was born in Paris in 1431. His real name was François de Montcorbier, but his father died while he was still a child and he was brought up by the canon, Guillaume de Villon, who sent him to study at the faculty of arts of at the University of Paris when he was twenty. He obtained his masters degree in 1452 and then he abandoned academe for an adventurous bohemian life. On 5 June 1455, as he was walking with his drinking companions, a violent brawl broke among himself, his friends and a priest, Philippe Chermoye - or perhaps Sermoise or Sermaise. Villon killed the priest with a sword and was banished from Paris. It was around that time that he wrote the poem generally known as the *Petit Testament*, although he had entitled it *Le Lais* (The Legacy), which is an ironic list of "bequests" to friends and acquaintances before leaving Paris. Actually, Villon's troubles were just starting. Pardoned, he returned to Paris six months later, but once again was forced to leave the city: with five companions he had robbed the Collège de Navarre. The rest of his life was punctuated with similar episodes. In the summer of 1461 he was arrested by order of Bishop Thibault d'Aussigny at Meung-sur-Loire for having robbed a church; on 2 October of the same year he was pardoned and released. He returned to Paris and barely had to time write *Le Testament* or *Le Grand Testament* before he was in trouble with the law again (1462), for theft and brawling. He was tortured, tried and condemned to be hanged, but on 5 January 1463 the sentence was commuted to banishment from Paris for 10 years, And there is no further record of François Villon after that date. *Le Testament* (1462) or *Le Grand Testament* as it is also known (to distinguish it from the *Lais*) is considered his masterpiece. It is a long, autobiographical poem of two thousand twenty-three lines in 186 eight-line stanzas interspersed with chansons and ballades including the *Ballade des dames du temps jadis* (Ballad of the Ladies of Bygone Times) with its reflections on the fleeting nature of female beauty. In contact with the thought of death we see his attachment to life. He sang of the women of Paris, he acknowledged the value of friendship and knelt in prayer at Notre-Dame. A keen observer and educated man, he wrote of themes that were essentially traditional for the period: regret for a wasted life, lost love, and the fear of death – a period of plagues, famines, massacres and war – and made great innovations in poetic form.

BEAUGENCY

Beaugency is a village between Beauce and Sologne, on the banks of the Loire. It is delightful to stroll along its characteristic streets flanked by an important group of civil and religious buildings erected between the 11th and 18th centuries (church of Notre Dame where two councils were held, the tower of St-Firmin, the Clock tower, the César tower, the Château Dunois, the house of the Templars, the town hall, the Tavers gate and the bridge over the Loire). On the site of the castle of the lords of Beaugency, built in the 11th century, the bastard of Orléans (illegitimate son of the Duke of Orléans Louis I and Marietta d'Enghien), built the castle after he became lord of Beaugency upon his marriage to Marie d'Harcourt. The castle belonged to the Dunois-Longueville family until 1789. Initially it was abandoned, then converted into a hospice for the poor and later into a regional holiday camp; now the castle is the **Regional Museum of Crafts and Traditions of the Orléans District**. It houses various collections (furniture, clothing and headwear, tools, toys, engravings, reconstructions of period interiors, etc.) that illustrate the customs of the region.

The Château Dunois is a typical 16th-century residence with double-light windows, a stairway tower and towers with arcading. The rooms have undergone major changes in the past two hundred years and only the garrets are in the original state. The impressive entrance façade, still bearing traces of the drawbridge, dates from the feudal period. The interior was entirely renovated in the 19th century and the twenty-one rooms are furnished in quite different styles: the Louis XIII room, Louis XV furniture, a Spanish dining room and an unusual 18th century bathroom with all its accessories. Underground are some cells and an interesting 12th-century chapel with a palm-shaped vault.

From top, the composite façade of the church of Notre-Dame and the sturdy 11th-century bastion next to the château.

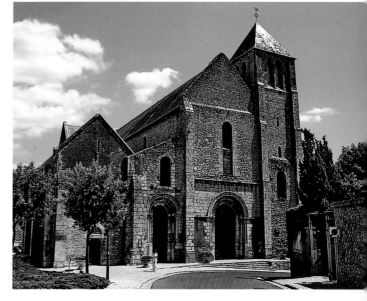

TALCY

The environs of the tiny village of Talcy in the heart of the Petite Beauce are both unusual and attractive. Indeed, beyond the historic castle flower and vegetable gardens lies the sweeping verdant countryside, for centuries cultivated with fields that stretch as far as the eye can see forming a kaleidoscope of fantastic shades and colours, with sunflowers, and

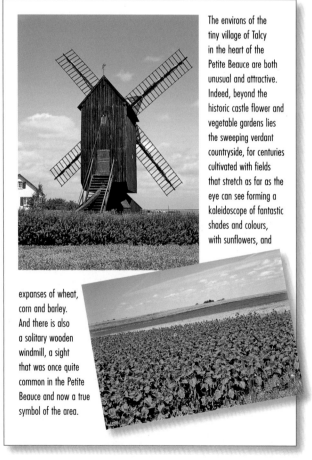

expanses of wheat, corn and barley. And there is also a solitary wooden windmill, a sight that was once quite common in the Petite Beauce and now a true symbol of the area.

The castle of Talcy is located in the centre of a charming village in the area of Beauce, a few kilometres from Mer. In 1517 Bernardo Salviati, a Florentine banker, member of the court of King Francis I and a relative of the Medici family, purchased the Talcy estate with "house, dovecot and annexes". In 1520 he received permission to convert Talcy into a "fortress-house". He added traditional feudal elements without, however, fortifying it: architecturally therefore, the building is archaic. On the death of Isabelle, the last of the Salviati line, the chateau passed to the Godet des Marais family. In 1780 Talcy was purchased by Gastebois, an ancestor of the last owner, and in 1932 ownership was transferred to the French state.

Cassandra, Bernardo Salviati's daughter lived in the castle; she was the first love of Ronsard, who sung her praises in *Les amours*. The castle is entered through a beautiful door set into a massive 15th-century tower with polygonal corner towers in brick and stone. There are neither drawbridges nor moats. The façade of the main building (east) is quite beautiful. The projecting wing was remodelled in the 18th century. A graceful Italian-style well enhances the first courtyard. A remarkably well-preserved 16th-century dovecot with 1500 compartments is in the second courtyard. In one of the outbuildings is a four hundred year-old press still in working order.

CHAMBORD

The château of Chambord is one of the loveliest Renaissance buildings in the valley of the Loire. The land on which it stands was the property of the Counts of Blois, of Champagne and of Chatillon from the 10th century on, until it was bought by Louis d'Orléans in 1392. When the new Duke of Orléans became king (as Louis XII) the county became the property of the crown. This elegant château was built by Francis I, Louis XII's successor, who came to the throne in 1515 when he was only 20 years old. Francis I, who was the son of Louise of Savoy, had been particularly impressed by the figure of Lorenzo the Magnificent, an outstanding personality in the field of politics and culture.

Above, painting attributed to the 18th-century French school: The Château of Chambord during the reign of Louis XV. Below, an aerial view of the château of Chambord, reveals the amazing symmetry of the structure.

The conquest of the territory of Milan provided Francis I with the opportunity of seeing the architecture of northern Italy. As a great patron of the arts and sciences, he succeeded in bringing Leonardo da Vinci to France. The king's wish to fuse the elements of Italian Renaissance architecture

Chambord

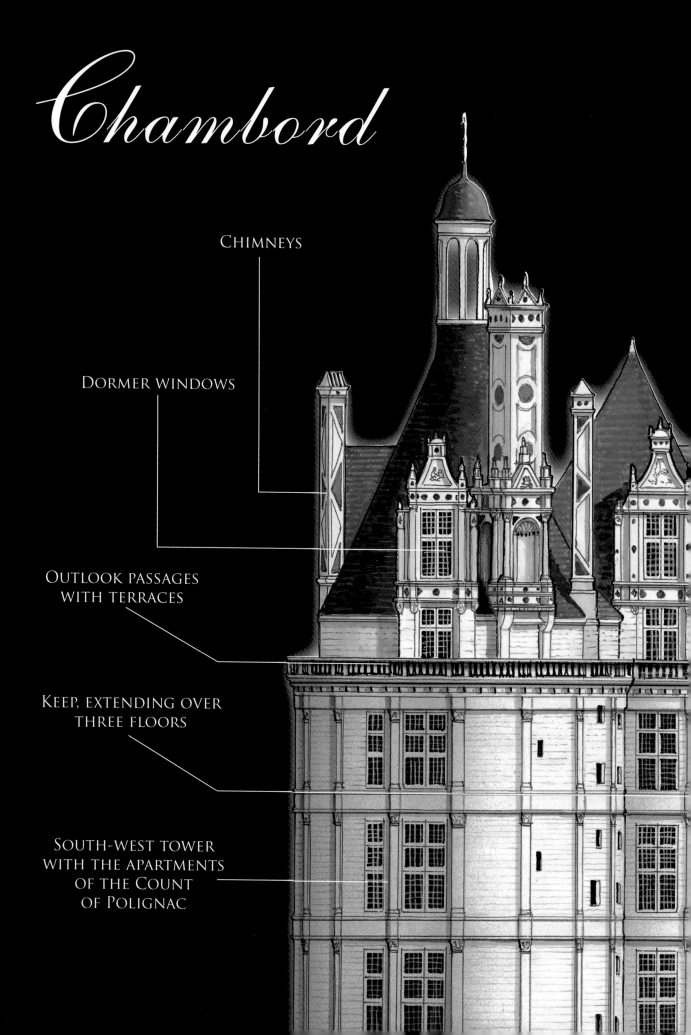

CHIMNEYS

DORMER WINDOWS

OUTLOOK PASSAGES
WITH TERRACES

KEEP, EXTENDING OVER
THREE FLOORS

SOUTH-WEST TOWER
WITH THE APARTMENTS
OF THE COUNT
OF POLIGNAC

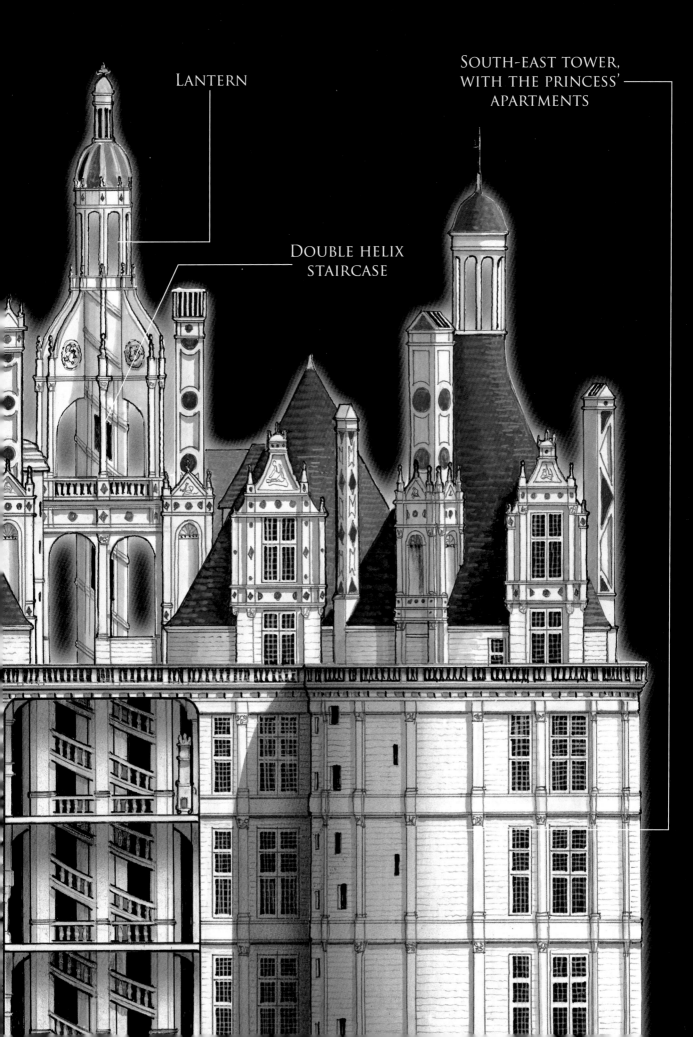

LANTERN

DOUBLE HELIX STAIRCASE

SOUTH-EAST TOWER, WITH THE PRINCESS' APARTMENTS

with those of the French tradition in a single building was partially granted when the château of Blois was enlarged. Leonardo da Vinci worked there too, in 1517, on a project for a castle that was never built. In 1519 he died in Clos-Lucé, near Amboise, it is said in the arms of Francis I who had hastened to his bedside. It was in that year that work on the large building, which was to become the king's country residence and hunting reserve, was begun on the estate of Chambord on the site of an older stronghold which had been demolished to make room for the new castle. All of 1800 men worked on the château and its additions from 1526 on.

The division of the floors into apartments that are separate but alike reveals the strong influence of contemporary Tuscan villas, while the large terraces and the magnificent spiral staircase at the centre of the cross bear Leonardo's mark. Although this type of staircase is derived from the medieval concept, it goes far beyond it in its unique division into two

separate flights with numerous openings on the arms of the corridors. A tribute to the former medieval French tradition is to be found in the presence of powerful cylindrical towers at the corners of the keep, which however harmonize with the building.

Construction work continued for many years. Around 1537 the keep was finished, in 1540 the two floors of the wing with the royal apartments were built, together with the ground floor of the wing with the chapel and the walls of the annexes, while it was not until 1547, when Francis I died, that the wing of the royal apartments was completed. The keep, seat of the royal court, had rooms arranged in a cross plan on each of its three floors and it was here that the social life of the courtiers took place. Balls were held on the second floor, where the ceilings of the rooms were enriched with coffering and vaulting. In the sectors contained within the arms of the cross there were four apartments per floor, in addition to another four in the corner towers. Each apart-

ment was just like the others: composed of a large hall as high as the whole floor and of two rooms, a study and a wardrobe, above which were rooms for service. Almost all the rooms (365 out of 440) had a fireplace so that each apartment could be independently heated.

The double spiral staircase in the centre, topped by a lantern, connected the various floors up to the top of the castle. The staircase is related to a project by Leonardo for a spiral stair which consisted of four distinct superimposed flights of stairs, in other words just as many stairs as quarters and arms of the cross in the castle. It is therefore likely that Leonardo da Vinci's staircase, which may have been conceived for Chambord, was then simplified when it was built by the master masons of the building site. The top of the stairs leads to the large roof terraces of the castle, which again reflect one of Leonardo's ideas, in which he intended them to be used as a place from which to admire the superstructures of the buildings. Along the walks which follow the cross plan, or those which skirt the perimeter of the wings and the towers, the members of the court could take walks and retire to observe the surrounding countryside and the hunts that were held there, as well as the decorations of the castle roof. As can be seen even from a distance, the upper part of the keep is crowded with dormer windows with Italianate classicizing superstructures, small towers, pavilions and elegant chimneys decorated with columns, clouds, miniature pediments, salamanders and geometric motifs in slate, applied to create a two-tone

Two picturesque views of the château, a masterpiece of French Renaissance architecture, with the detail of the terrace and the elaborate rooftops.

effect similar to that of Italian monuments decorated with polychrome marble. The upper part of the lantern, which surmounts the spiral staircase, rises 32 metres into the air. Originally open – the glass was added later – the upper part is supported by projecting rounded arches of medieval origin. The sculpture inside the keep, executed between 1525 and 1550, displays the profound influence of Italian classical art.

A floor plan such as that of the keep, which provided for apartments that were all alike, was not suitable for the royal apartments, which had to be larger and more sumptuous. With this in mind, the two wings for the king's rooms and for the chapel were added in 1526. Although they could obviously not have been foreseen in the original plan, the new sections seem an integral part of the keep in their style, concept and proportions. In fact these later wings used the side of the keep as the unit of measure: it was multiplied by three and by two respectively for the width and depth of the new buildings.

The royal apartments, situated in the northeast

The Francis I wing of the château and, below, the large central double spiral staircase supported by four pillars culminating in a skylight.

corner and in part conceived like the others, had two extra rooms. One, which was very large and long, was the official audience hall, illuminated by rows of windows like some of the rooms in the palace of Fontainebleau. The other room, more intimate and reached by means of a staircase, was a private study in Italian Renaissance style. There were two walls with windows and a coffered ceiling decorated with carvings of salamanders and the initial F of Francis I.

The chapel, situated to the northwest, was also profoundly influenced by Italian art and through this, by classic art: double Doric columns and pediments are combined with a large barrel vault (which in the original project had the usual coffering). The plan of the castle, in its absolute symmetry, can be symbolically interpreted: the keep, seat of the court with standardized apartments, is set between the wing of Francis I and that of the chapel; that is, between the king and God. Other theories, based on the observation of the park, go even further and interpret the large trees in the woods as a symbol of the people and the circular enclosing walls of the estate, 33 kilometres long, as the symbol of the boundaries of France. Life and activity within the castle took place principally in the rooms in the arms of the cross and on the stair-

From the top, the staircase in typical Renaissance style, and the vaulted ceiling of the Guardroom, with the initials and symbol - the salamander - of Francis I.

cases. In moving from one floor to another and from one apartment to another, the courtiers used the central staircase and the rooms as well as the loggias which lead to the corner towers. In moving about between the floors, it was also possible to use the spiral staircases which cut through the thickness of the corner towers and not only put the floors and landings of the apartments in communication, but also led to the bathrooms on the ground floor. Francis I, together with his wife Eleanor, his mistress Anne de Pisseleu and the court, resided off and on in Chambord. Besides various official encounters, the king usually went there for a few weeks every two years for hunting. On the other hand, in addition to his many official obligations, he had many other hunting lodges to choose from. The considerable quantity of furnishings he brought in his wake remained in the castle only as long as the king was there. Among these were trunks, chests, bunk beds and wall hangings, including many tapestries which decorated the walls and made the rooms warmer. In the winter of 1539, when Charles V came to stay in the castle, the Baron of Montmorency (grand master of ceremonies) installed a particularly luxuriant interior decoration. The emperor, who it is said was preceded by maidens who threw flower petals in his path, admired the castle and defined it, together with the objects it contained, as "a synthesis of what human industry can accomplish". Francis I, who was a connoisseur of women, included 27 young ladies of rank in his household and many more in that of the queen. Indeed, he said "a court without women is like a year without spring and a spring without roses". Even so, in the autumn of 1545 the melancholy king wrote the words "woman is fickle, unhappy he who trusts her" on a window

Above, the dauphine's room, on the first floor and, right, details of the embroidered tapestries; facing page above, the bedroom of Francis I and the queen's bedroom, below, the monumental bed in the room where Louis XIV slept.

pane with his diamond ring. When Francis I died the royal residence moved to Paris. His son and successor Henry II however continued work on Chambord, realizing the second floor of the chapel and all those structures decorated with a sculpted H, his emblem. In 1552 the treaty which united the three bishoprics of Toul, Metz and Verdun, which he had previously occupied, was signed here. On his death in 1559 work on the castle stopped, although Catherine de' Medici continued to frequent the palace together with her children. Charles IX was particularly fond of hunting and many tales are told about his prowess as a hunter and a rider. It is said that he was able to follow a deer until it was exhausted without using his dogs. After his death in 1574 the castle was practically unused for about fifty years, since Henry III and Henry IV rarely resided there. In 1626 Louis XIII gave his brother Gaston d'Orléans the county of Blois which included the château of Chambord. Actually this gift seems not to have been dictated so much by motives of brotherly

love as by the desire to free himself of doubts as to Gaston's loyalty. The new owner immediately began to repair the residence. The tale is told of how in playing with his daughter, of whom he was particularly fond, Gaston d'Orléans agreed to climb up and down one of the flights of the large spiral staircase while his daughter ran up and down the other without ever meeting him. Later the château once again became part of the property of the crown and Louis XIV, even though he stayed there only nine times, began important works of restoration and transformation. He abandoned Francis I's original royal wing and moved into new apartments refurbished for him at the front of the castle. New rooms on the first floor and luxurious furnishings arrived to enrich the castle from 1680 on, together with the addition of a new entrance with a pediment. The estate itself, which up to then had been covered with natural vegetation, was in part redeveloped into parks.

In 1669 Molière and Lulli wrote *Monsieur de Pourceaugnac* here and it was first presented privately for the king. It is recalled that because the leading actor was indisposed Lulli himself agreed to replace him at the last moment so as not to deprive the king of the show. Despite the fact that Lulli acted well

A few of the portraits conserved in the château's gallery: facing page, from the top and the left, Louis XIII, Henry IV, Louis XIV and Charles X; this page, above, Louis XV and the Dauphine Marie Antoinette; left, Françoise d'Aubigné.

and that there were plenty of comic situations, he noticed that Louis XIV was not laughing. Not even the lively scene of the druggists succeeded in getting the king to smile. At this point, improvising, Lulli quickly jumped off the stage, got a running start and landed with both feet on the harpsichord, smashing it to smithereens with a great racket. At this comic situation the king

The interior of the chapel, completed for Louis XIV by Jules Hardouin-Mansart.

burst out laughing, clapping and thus determining the success of the play. The next year another work by Molière, *Le Bourgeois Gentilhomme* was presented in the castle.

It is said that around this time, here in the castle, Anne Marie Louise d'Orleans declared her love to the Duc de Lauzun by writing the name of her beloved on a mirror after having clouded the surface with her breath. Louis XIV's new preoccupations, above all the war, put a halt to the work. It was later carried on by Stanislao Leszczynski, to whom the manor had been given by his son-in-law Louis XV in 1725. Twenty years later the castle became the property of Marshal de Saxe, the victor of Prague, Fontenoy, Rocourt and Lawfeld. The king explicitly requested that the volunteers of De Saxe's regiment be quartered in the castle.

These included Poles, Hungarians, Turks and Tartars in flashy uniforms as well as the "colonel company" of negros from Martinique mounted on white Ucrainian horses. In 1750 Marshal de Saxe mysteriously died. It is said that it was not pneumonia but rather that he fell in a duel with the Prince of Conti because of the latter's wife. After his death the castle cannons were fired every quarter of an hour for six days as a sign of mourning.

After having passed through a succession of owners, the château risked being demolished after the Revolution, and in 1793 the furnishings were dispersed.

The castle continued to be in a critical state under Napoleon's empire when it belonged to Marshal Berthier and successively to the Duke of Bordeaux. During a visit, Gustave Flaubert wrote particularly haunting lines at the sight of the empty rooms "where the spider weaves its web on the salamander of Francis I".

Despite various attempts at restoration, such as the restoration of the lantern and all the beams, the building continued in its precarious state until 1947, when the State began restorations which continued for decades. The rooms of the château open to the public today con-

A beautiful "Polish style" bed, with its vivid tapestries, in the apartments refurbished in 1785 for the Marquis of Polignac.

The bedroom of the Count of Chambord - the sculptured wood bed was made in 1873 by Emile Poinçon - still preserves the battery of miniature cannons the young Duke of Bordeaux used to play with.

tain various furnishings, including tapestries in the rooms of Louis XIV, and paintings, including the portraits of Henry III and Anne of Austria. Other rooms contain objects which belonged to the Duke of Bordeaux, the Count of Chambord and last legitimate claimant to the throne of France. These include a bed and a toy battery of cannons in miniature. The ground floor contains an exhibit of the carriages built by Hermès in 1871 and which were never used. They were to have served the Count of Chambord in making his entrance into the capital to accede to the throne.

Blois

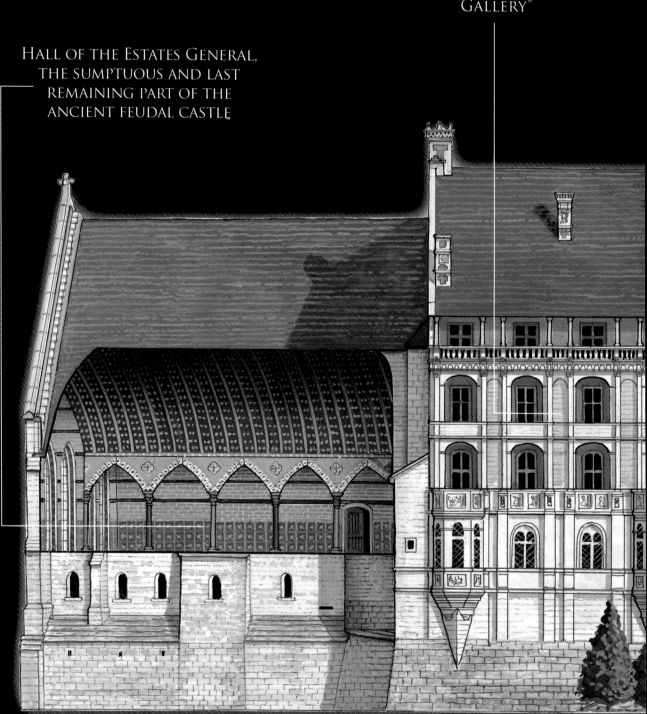

LOGGIAS
CORRESPONDING
TO THE "QUEEN'S
GALLERY"

HALL OF THE ESTATES GENERAL,
THE SUMPTUOUS AND LAST
REMAINING PART OF THE
ANCIENT FEUDAL CASTLE

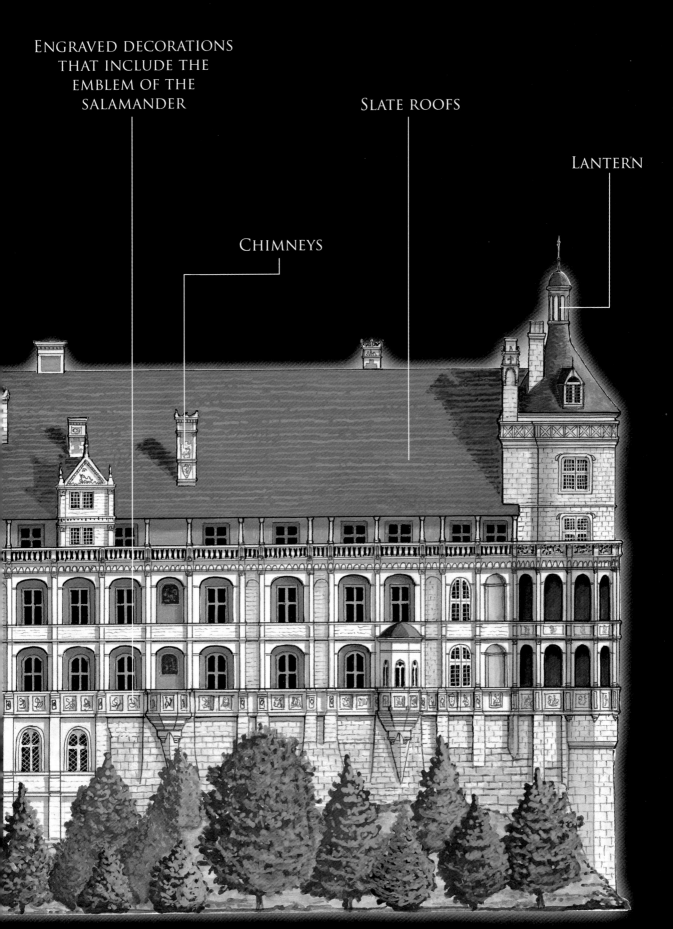

ENGRAVED DECORATIONS
THAT INCLUDE THE
EMBLEM OF THE
SALAMANDER

SLATE ROOFS

LANTERN

CHIMNEYS

FAÇADES OF THE LOGGIAS

This regal city on the Loire is rich in monuments, history and culture. It was the birthplace of Louis XII (1462), Denis Papin, who first conceived of the steam engine (1647), and J. N. Augustin Thierry, French historian (1795).
Built in the XVI century, but destroyed by a hurricane in 1678, the **Cathédrale St-Louis** was reconstructed in the Gothic style towards the end of the 17th century. It is flanked by a tall Renaissance tower with a domed top. The crypt dates from the 10th-11th centuries. The **St-Nicolas Church** was built between the 12th and 13th centuries. The building is considered one of the finest blends of Romanesque and Gothic architecture.

BLOIS

Even thousands of years ago the exceptional lie of the land around Blois was well-known – a rocky promontory hollowed out by the junction of the Loire and a stream made it easy to isolate and defend. It was no doubt used as early as the Neolithic Age, even though the existence of the castle was not documented until the 9th century.

Towards the middle of the 10th century, Blois and the surrounding countryside were given in fief to very powerful noblemen, the Counts of Blois, vassals of the King of France and also counts of Tours, Chartres and later of Champagne: they rebuilt the fortified castle several times. The only remaining evidence of the imposing fortress built during the 13th century are a corner tower, fragments of ramparts and towers incorporated here and there in later constructions; and above all, the large assembly room and ballroom of the Counts of Blois.

At the end of the 14th century, the county of Blois was sold to Prince Louis of Orléans, son of the King of France, Charles V, initiating a brilliant future for the town. His son, the poet Charles of Orléans, lived in the castle for 25 years after his return from serving a long prison sentence in England, attracting a small court of scholars and poets around him. But of even greater importance for the town, his grandson became King of France in 1498 under the name of Louis XII, following the accidental death in Amboise of his cousin, the young Charles VIII, who died leaving no heirs. Born in Blois, Louis XII decided to establish his residence there. Thus, the small town of Blois became the royal town and capital of the kingdom during part of the 16th century. It was a most fortunate choice, as the town and region were rapidly expanding at the time and all their inhabitants were devoted to the Dukes of Orléans who had brought them so much prosperity.

At the time of Charles of Orléans, and especially under Louis XII and Francis I, the town of Blois grew considerably. But after the death of Queen Claude of France in 1524 and the disaster of Pavia in 1525, Francis I never returned to Blois and his successors only paid short visits to the town. During the 17th century, the city was brought back to life by the prolonged stay (1634-1660) of Gaston d'Orléans, brother of Louis XIII.

Facing page, a general view of Blois extending along the banks of the Loire.
Below, an aerial view of the town and the château with, right, a view of the famous Loggia Façade of the Francis I wing.

The Gothic-style equestrian statue of Louis XII, in the internal courtyard of the Louis XII wing.

The Louis XII wing, which originally extended on three sides of the court, was built rapidly in the space of three years. The new appearance of this gracious manor, built in brick and stone, is surprising. It is devoid of the towers and battlements which were still widespread during that period and the large windows, balconies, skylights and open galleries let in a great deal of air and light. The architecture of Louis XII's wing is serene, gay and gracious, in keeping with a king who was known for his simple, affable manner. It was no longer a fortified castle because Louis XII did not need to defend himself; his power was undisputed. By now, the King of France required a castle of government which could be used for receptions and balls. The king introduced a new way of governing, an "open" diplomacy inspired by the Italians, as can be seen from the revolutionary diplomatic act represented by the sumptuous reception held in 1501 in the castle of Blois in honour of the Archduke of Austria with whom France was practically at war. If Louis XII's constructions were modern in design, they remained basically Gothic in many aspects: lack of regularity and symmetry in their plan and distribution of

The kings paid little attention to the château of Blois throughout the 18th century. It was divided into small apartments and used to house old servants of the Crown. The gardens were parcelled out and it fell into a state of general neglect. In 1788, Louis XVI ordered the sale of the castle or failing that, its demolition. It was saved by its transformation into a military barracks.

During and after the Revolution, various monuments of Blois were mutilated, or even destroyed stone by stone. The castle did not escape these acts of vandalism and all the emblems and effigies of the royal family were effaced. During the first half of the 19th century, the castle was modified due to military occupation.

In 1845 the architect Duban began a radical restoration of the château which is now considered to have been excessive.

Louis XII wing. In 1498, Louis Duke of Orléans and Count of Blois became King of France under the name of Louis XII. The new king soon undertook to rebuild his ancestors' castle.

Facing page, above, the internal courtyard (1498-1501) of the Louis XII wing; below, the Francis I wing, with its monumental staircase.

openings; fine, sharp-pointed, hollowed-out mouldings and rich, sculpted decorations, consisting, as in the cathedrals, of friezes of foliage, pinnacles and rosettes and in particular, of corbels with picturesque personages in very Medieval vein. According to French and Gothic tradition, the initials and emblems of the owners of the place are sculpted in the stone: fleur-de-lis for the king and ermine spots for the queen, Anne de Bretagne, on the columns of the gallery; porcupines, emblems of the Dukes of Orléans, on the Great Staircase ("De près comme de loin, je suis redoutable!"). An equestrian statue of the king crowns the main entrance of the château. The gallery set against the chapel of which the southern half was destroyed during the 19th century was for many years wrongfully attributed to Charles of Orléans when it really was one of Louis XII's constructions. The greater restraint of this building is not at all surprising as it was a simple corridor connecting two main buildings and not a residential wing. The façade of the chapel, decorated with the initials of Louis XII and Queen Anne de Bretagne, was remade during the 19th century. The interior is entirely in Gothic style with pointed arch vaulting, keystones and tiles with heraldic decorations.

Francis I wing. In the great number of constructions undertaken by Francis I, a prince "marvellously dedicated to buildings", Blois was the first in chronological order: the Francis I wing was commenced in 1515, that is at the beginning of his reign, and work was completed before 1524, marking the death of Queen Claude of France, whose initials and emblems are associated everywhere with those of the king. Built only 15 years after the Louis XII wing, the Francis I wing is very different. During these 15 years, French art changed radically through contact with Italian art. The Francis I wing is one of the very first masterpieces of the French Renaissance. The overall appearance of the façade looking on to the courtyard is Gothic in style on account of the lack of symmetry and due to the traditional French animation of the upper parts of the building. The steep slate roof is embellished by large chimney stacks and imposing skylights and emphasized by an openwork balustrade. But the decorative system is completely new: the windows are framed by pilasters continuing from one level to another. As a concession to tradition, the emblem of the king, the salamander (whose motto means: "I encourage good and I stifle evil"), is sculpted eleven times in high relief on the

Facing page, the room "of the two fireplaces", in the Francis I wing of the château, with Renaissance style furniture and with the monumental fireplace dating from the days of Francis I. Right, in detail, the symbols of the King and of Queen Claude of France: the salamander and the ermine.

Facing page, above, the royal apartments in the Francis I wing with gilded leather wall coverings; below, a room in the Museum of Fine Arts housed in the former apartments of Louis XII.

Above, the room of the Estates General.

Francis I façade. The staircase, which was at the centre of the façade before Gaston d'Orléans began to modify the château, is a masterpiece. When the Italianate straight flights of stairs appeared in the Loire Valley after the Gothic period, the shape of the spiral staircase in a protruding octagonal cage was considered rather ordinary. The originality of the solution adopted here lies in the lattice-work of the walls between the corner buttresses. This staircase, with its three floors of balconies looking on to the Court of Honour, was perfectly suited to the pomp of the increasingly sumptuous royal ceremonies. **Gaston d'Orléans wing.** The structure at the back of the courtyard was built between 1635 and 1638 for Gaston d'Orléans, Louis XIII's brother, exiled to Blois due to his perpetual intrigues against the king.
Nowdays the Gaston d'Orléans wing houses the municipal library and two large halls used for concerts, conferences and exhibitions.

Francis I wing, interior. On ascending the famous staircase to enter the Francis I wing, one notices the repetition of curved lines in the shape of the stairs, handrail, cornices and ribbed vault. The medallions of this vault bear the initials and emblems of Francis I, of his wife Claude of France (the "C" and the ermine), and of his mother Louise of Savoy (the swan pierced by an arrow, the crossed wings). The first hall one enters on the first floor is formed by two halls joined together during restoration in the mid-19th century. The Francis I apartments were largely restored during that period by the architect Duban: the tile flooring was redone and the walls and beams were repainted. Over a period of fifteen years, the Francis I wing was gradually renovated and furnished: Italian style tables, Flemish tapestries, chairs and, above all, chests which continued to be the basic piece of furniture during the Renaissance as in the Middle Ages. The second hall, known as the "room of the guards", features

an extraordinarily large piece of embroidery dating to the 17th century and portraying religious subjects. Two oft-reproduced portraits of the poet Ronsard, one painted and the other sculpted, can also be seen. In fact, tradition has it that it was at the castle of Blois during a ball that Ronsard met Cassandra Salviati to whom he dedicated so many poems. A wooden panel dating to the second half of the 16th century depicts a ball at the court of the Valois which could have taken place in Blois. It mainly represents the volta, an Italian dance introduced by Catherine de' Medici. The old building's medieval structure can clearly be seen on passing from that hall to the following gallery: the door recess in the 2 metre-thick rampart and rounded sections of the tower to the right on entering. The gallery itself was also built by Francis I and opens outward mainly through kinds of loggias, variants of the loggias of Bramante at the Vatican, which in the past overlooked vast gardens.

The royal busts assembled in this gallery are a reminder of the long visits paid by Catherine de' Medici and her children to the castle of Blois during the last third of the XVI century and of the interest paid by their successor, King Henry IV, to the castle of Blois where he had a 200 metre-long gallery built along the edge of the gardens; unfortunately, however, it fell into ruin during the 18th century. At the back of the gallery one can admire a Spanish or Portuguese "Bargueño", in the numerous drawers of which precious

Above left, the canopied bed where Catherine de' Medici died on 5 January 1589; above right, the door and boiseries of the oratory that leads to the private study of Catherine de' Medici (top, with its wood panels).

collections were stowed away. After the ante-room in an old tower dating back to the 13th century set against the rampart (note the thickness of the four walls of this room), one enters the royal bedroom occupied on several occasions by Catherine de' Medici, forced to flee from Paris which was shaken by religious troubles at the time. She died there on 5th January 1589, a matter of days after the Duke of Guise was assassinated. This room, thus named Cath-

erine de' Medici's bedroom, was decorated with the initials of Henry II and of the queen when it was restored during the 19th century. During the 16th century, the room was not as private as one is made to believe nowadays. Guests were happily received there. The recess in the wall no doubt enhanced the importance of the

Right, the assassination of the Duke of Guise in paintings by Paul Delaroche.

Below, the bedroom of King Henry III where the Duke of Guise was assassinated on 23 December 1588.

Above, the gallery corresponding to the Loggia façade, with the busts of Charles IX, Henry II, Henry III and Henry IV.
Left, two rooms that were part of the apartments of Louis XII and now host the Museum of Fine Arts.

chair set on a small platform and sheltered under a dais where the queen sat. Various pieces of furniture recreate the atmosphere of a bedroom. The portraits on the walls are a reminder of Catherine de' Medici's preference for the art of portaiture the development of which she encouraged during the 16th century. The nearby chapel features interesting painted woodwork and, in the apse, one can admire an attractive piece of sculpture. The study is the most interesting room in the Francis I wing as it has kept its original carved wainscoting: 237 panels, which are all different, offer a complete repertory of the decorative motifs used at the beginning of the Renaissance: arabesques, horns of plenty, masks, dolphins, etc. This room is likewise famous on account of its secret wall-cupboards known as "poison" cupboards as in a novel by Alexandre Dumas. But it is not known, in fact, whether Catherine de' Medici, ever hid poison there! While the second floor of the Francis I wing was being renovated it was the scene of a tragic event which occupies an important place in French history. On the 23rd of December 1588, Henry, Duke of Guise, was assassinated by order of King Henry III of France. This assassination was the outcome of religious strife that ravaged France during the reigns of the children of Henry II and of Catherine de' Medici initiated by the fanaticism of the Protestants supported by Elizabeth of England and the intransigence of the Catholics, reunited in the bosom of the League, and encouraged by Philip II of Spain. The authority of the king was perpetually challenged by this League, and in particular by its head, the Duke of Guise. The situation worsened during the meeting of the Estates General of the kingdom at the castle of Blois in October 1588: Henry of Guise took over and openly ridiculed the king, who resolved to assassinate him. The pictures in the Cabinet room and in the king's bedroom illustrate this tragic event as well as the assassination of the Cardinal of Lorraine, brother of the Duke of Guise, which took place 24 hours later. On returning to the first floor, one reaches the hall of the Estates General. This was the great hall of the fortress of the Counts of Blois, built at the beginning of the 13th century. It was in this hall – one of the oldest still extant in a Gothic castle – that the Count of Blois exercised his authority, dispensed justice and received the homage of his vassals. While it was part of the royal

castle, it housed on two occasions, under Henry III in 1576 and 1588, the Estates General of the kingdom of France. The arrangement of this hall with its two naves separated by a row of columns recalls the chapter-house of an abbey. The capitals date it to the beginning of the 13th century. The naves are not covered by stone vaults but by a panelled ceiling consisting of small planks of wood juxtaposed. The interior decoration was repainted during the 19th century.

Left, France resembling Maria de' Medici, *of the Rubens school.*
Above right, Allegory of Love *(16th century)*; Death of Adonis, *by Martin de Vos.*

BEAUREGARD

The castle of Beauregard, between Bois and Cheverny is situated on the edge of the Russy forest and is surrounded by a large park.

Originally, Jean Doulcet, a former Master of the Chamber to Charles of Orléans, lived there in 1495. René, bastard of Savoy and uncle to Francis I, received this estate as a gift in 1529 from his royal nephew. In 1545 the poet Jean du Thier, protector of Ronsard and Du Bellay, secretary to King Hen-

ry II, bought this hunting lodge for two thousand gold écus and transformed it into a castle. In 1617 the property was purchased by Paul Ardier, treasurer to three kings (Henry III, Henry IV and Louis XIII). Afterwards, it changed hands several times and was owned by the Fieubert family, the Marquis de Gaucourt, the Viscount de Préval in 1816, the Countess of Ste-Aldegonde in 1850, the Count of Cholet, Louis Thillier, and then, in 1907 it became the property of the De Gosselin family, grandparents of the current owners, M. and Mme du Cheyron du Pavillon.

The castle hosted many important guests. Francis I stayed at the hunting lodge. In 1626 Richelieu preferred Beauregard to Blois which was considered unsafe and ideal for plotters, and the duchess of Montpensier stayed there several times.

Over the centuries the castle was modified considerably. The original residence was enlarged in 1545 by Jean du Their, secretary of state to Henry II, in 1545 with the hunting lodge, two parallel structures connected by two superposed galleries, flanked by two pavilions. In 1617 the old building was demolished. Ardier ordered the construction of two, lower symmetrical wings and began work on the Portrait

Above, the main façade of the castle.
To the left, the charming south Gallery.

Gallery. In the 19th century the Marquis of Gaucourt demolished the north wing, the chapel and the frescoes by Nicolò dell'Abate. An English park was laid out. The Countess of Ste-Aldegonde doubled the western gallery and added a neo-Gothic ora-

Right, the Portrait Gallery, with portraits of the illustrious men from the courts of twelve kings of France, from Philip VI to Louis XIII (bottom, a detail). Below, the Cabinet des Grelots, with its precious gilded lining.

tory which no longer exists. In 1850 the architect Jules de la Morandière restored the castle and especially the southern wing which was returned to its 16th-century dimensions.

In 1902 Thillier began new restorations, raising the roofs and unifying the east and west façades in the Renaissance style. Today, a chateau of moderate dimensions, Beauregard still has the charm of a 16th-century residence. The current owners have also restored the annexes to their 17th-century appearance. The chateau's Portrait Gallery is of particular interest. It still has the original Delft tile floor (depicting infantry and cavalry troops on parade), boiserie and a ceiling with paintings by Pierre Mosnier. The gallery contains 363 portraits from the first of the Valois to Louis XIII (kings, queens, courtiers, ministers and famous personalities). The Cabinet des Grelots, or room of the bells, created in the 16th century, is entirely covered by sculpted gilt decorations by Francisque Scibec de Carpi.

CHEVERNY

What strikes one most about Cheverny at first sight are its majesty and symmetry. It consists of a tall building with square pavilions joining two wings covered by rounded roofs surmounted by lanterns. Its Renaissance architecture has been clearly influenced by the classical period; this can be seen from the series of niches with busts decorating the façade.

Unlike other castles, such as Blois and Chambord, whose interiors are almost empty, Cheverny boasts magnificent, intact furnishings dating back to the period of Louis XIII. In fact the castle has benefited from the rare privilege of having always belonged to the same family (except for a brief period in 1564 when Diane de Poitiers lived there), and this has produced a great unity of taste and style.

We know that in 1315 the castle of Cheverny was a simple mill. At the time, the Hurault family was already famous; from father to son, they were secretaries, ministers and chancellors under various sovereigns, from Louis XII to Henry IV. In 1490 Jacques Hurault, Louis XII's intendant, decided to transform the mill into a castle; this gave rise to a building "with a moat, drawbridge, turrets, barbicans and other forms of defence". This castle, of which only a drawing remains, appears to have been built where the outbuildings stand at present.

The elegant façade of Cheverny.

Left, the Guards' Room, with the magnificent Renaissance fireplace.

Below left, the dining room with its Cordova leather covered walls and, right, the royal bedroom with its coffered ceiling decorated by Jean Mosnier and the elegant 16th-century canopied bed upholstered in Persian silk.

Facing page, a portrait of Philippe Hurault Count of Cheverny (1525-1599) chancellor to the king, and of Elizabeth Hurault Marquise of Montglas (1645-1695) dressed for the hunt.

A document relates that the existing castle, built in 1634, was erected "on the site of the previous one", but it is not clear whether the phrase "on the site" means "on the same site" or "in place of". In any case, Cheverny's history is connected to a famous, dismal event, as related in the *Memories* of the Marquis Durfort de Cheverny, a historian who lived in the castle during the Revolution. Henri Hurault inherited the estate in 1599 at the age of 24. At a very young age, he had married the eleven-year-old Françoise Chabot, but the couple had lived almost always apart because of the long military campaigns in which Henri participated. One day as a young man he was in Paris at King Henry IV's court; as a joke, he raised two fingers to look like horns above Henry's head. His gesture was met with laughter but a mirror revealed to the count that he himself was the laughing stock. Without saying a word, the young man mounted on horseback and rode until he arrived home at dawn. In great silence, the count had the doors opened and arrived unexpectedly in his wife's

A Gobelin tapestry depicting the Abduction of Helen of Troy *(17th century).*

Below, a Louis XIV chest.

bedroom; the story goes that the young page with whom the countess consoled herself over her husband's long absences jumped out a window just in time, breaking a leg. The count killed him with his sword. Then, accompanied by a priest, he returned to his wife's bedroom, holding a glass of poison in one hand and a sword in the other, and told her that he would return within an hour, leaving the anguished woman to make the terrible decision. When the time was up, the count returned; his wife drank the poison and died. This must have been more or less how the story went, as the parish register of St-Martin de Blois certainly gives a truthful picture. In fact, it is stated that "On Saturday 26th January... the Countess of Cheverny was poisoned because

she committed adultery and rumour has it that when the surgeons, William and son, opened her, they discovered a five and a half month old child, the same day a gentleman from Burgundy called Chambelin, suspected of being her lover, was killed in the said castle of Cheverny." No matter what really happenend, it remains certain that Henri Hurault, having accomplished his terrible mission, returned to Paris the same evening in time for the "coucher du roi" ceremony. When the king heard about the sad events for which in fact he was mainly responsible, he became most irritated and exiled the count for three years to the Cheverny estate. Here Henri Hurault fell in love with the daughter of his Knight Commander and married her; it was his second wife, described as being thrifty, intelligent and with great taste, who directed the

Right, the empire style library.

Left, the dining room in the private apartments.

works, enlarging and embellishing the castle; for this purpose, she commissioned the architect Bohier and the artist Jean Mosnier. A direct descendant of the Huraults, the Marquis of Vibraye then handed on the tradition to his grandchildren, the Viscount and Viscountess of Sigalas, who inherited the estates on his death and who still today keep Cheverny's past splendour intact.

Left, the 17th-century grand staircase.

The castle's outbuildings house an exceptional Trophy room, containing a collection of over two thousand deer antlers, and a kennel housing a sixty-strong pack trained for coursing. The owners of Cheverny regularly organize hunts, which are greatly appreciated in hunting circles.

The Orangery

Built at the beginning of the 18th century to the right of the main castle structure, the orangery is an elegant building, simple but sophisticated in the purity of the architectural style. It has recently been carefully restored and renovated, and is now an ideal and convenient venue for conferences, seminars and other prestigious events. Fearing that Paris might be bombed during the Second World War, many works of art from the Louvre were stored here, including the famous painting of the *Mona Lisa*.

TROUSSAY

The castle originated in the 15th century. In 1546, the first known owner of record was Robert Bugy, comptroller of the salt stores at Blois and the king's equerry. His descendents lived in the castle until the 18th century. In 1732 Troussay was purchased by the Pelluys family. In 1828 the castle was inherited by the historian Louis de la Saussaye. With the help of the architect de la Morandière he undertook the rescue of Troussay which was in "great disrepair" and the restoration undertaken "scrupulously respected the manor's proportions and physiognomy". Prosper Merimée later stayed at the castle.

The northern façade develops around a 19th-century tower with stairway, which is decorated with a porcupine, symbol of Louis XII. The two long structures of the annexes in the entrance courtyard lend the manor the air of a traditional Sologne country house.

The interior of the castle was considerably restored during the 19th century. Note the external additions: coloured windows from the Sardini and Guise palaces at Blois (16th century), the dancing cupids painted in grisaille by Jean Mosnier (17th century) and the exceptional example of early Renaissance ornamental sculpture on the door of the Bury chapel. The annexes host a **Museum of the Crafts and Traditions of Sologne**, that illustrates the various aspects of rural life in this region.

The castle of Troussay, with the typical small tower.

LE ROUJOUX
THE "ENCHANTED CASTLE" OF FRESNES

The castle of Roujoux is located in the town of Fresnes, between Fougères-sur-Bièvre and Contres.
In 1080 Marie Frangal, daughter of the lord of Fougères was the first mistress of Roujoux. Between 1315 and 1440 Roujoux was divided into five small feifs that belonged to the castle of Blois. In 1450 Guillaume Paris reunited these five fiefs and described the estate as consisting of "one tile-covered house, another house that serves as a barn and a courtyard between them", surrounded by moats filled with water. In 1528 Jacques des Pas de Feuquières sold Roujoux to Jean de Villebresme, chamberlain to the king. In 1549 Pierre de Villebresme built the left wing of the existing castle. In 1618 René de Maille-Benehart, gentleman of the King's Chamber, and Master of the Hunt in the county of Maine, rebuilt Roujoux and maintained the Villebresme residence in one wing. In 1777 the building, which then belonged to Louis Richou de Rochefort, was in extremely poor condition, though it was spared total destruction by the Revolution. In 1818 the property was divided up: the castle had

9 owners in less than 70 years! In 1827 the chapel was eliminated. In 1830 Colonel Carrel entrusted the castle to Binet a former officer of the Royal Guards who demolished the entrance gate, drawbridge and one of the towers in the garden. In 1889 Roujoux was purchased by Gabriel de la Morandière, son of the architect who worked on the restorations at Blois and Chaumont.
Inside, in the gallery one can see a lovely 17th-century fireplace. The painted doors and wall decorations were done by Gabriel de la Morandière (19th century). The rooms are enlivened by automatons that tell the stories of the *Thousand and One Nights*, an evening with the harpsichord, and the history of the castle, complete with sound.

The park

A lovely wooded park, the river, meadows, and moats give the entire area around the chateau a tranquil country charm which is enlivened by barnyard animals, an aviary, peacocks, etc.
This intriguing chateau is referred to as the "enchanted castle" for, as well as the entertainment it offers inside and the animals that constitute one of France's zoological gardens, numerous outdoor play facilities for children are available in the grounds.

Meadows and moats in the tranquil countryside around Roujoux.

FOUGÈRES-SUR-BIÈVRE

Like the other châteaux of the Loire, Fougères is also situated on the area of a medieval stronghold with external defenses. During the Hundred Years' War the castle was the scene of military action and the Black Prince destroyed a great part of it and all the defensive

structures. Later, in 1470, the new owner was Pierre de Refuge, who held the offices of counselor for Charles of Orléans and then treasurer to the royal court under Louis XI. Economically well off, Pierre was able to undertake the reconstruction of the area around the central keep which the ravages of time and man had left fairly intact. The defensive walls and the circular towers which still flank the central part were thus completed, although not by Pierre but by his successor, his son-in-law Jean de Villebresme. As can be noted from the internal courtyard, the complex still bears signs of its medieval origin, untouched by the Italian Renaissance influences of the early 16th century. The towers are illuminated internally only by small windows – in line with the parameters of military structures – and are covered by steep conical slate roofs. The walls of irregular stones and mortar differ from the more elegant structures that became fashionable later with perfectly cut stone blocks. The low heavy arches of the courtyard lend a feeling of strength and sobriety, quite unlike the refined elegance introduced into French architecture by King Francis I when he returned from Italy. The presence of orifices for throwing molten lead, strong walls and defensive moats demonstrate that the castle was still thought of as a stronghold and not yet as a pleasant residence, pleasing to behold and hospitable inside. Not until the 16th century were new wide windows cut into the walls of the rooms which had enormous fireplaces. In the nearby town is the small church which still preserves many Romanesque features despite more recent additions.

The fortified château of Fougères-sur-Bièvre, one of the last examples of feudal architecture.

LASSAY-SUR-CROISNE

In an isolated setting in the midst of green lawns and beautiful trees, this castle was built by Philippe du Moulin between 1480 and 1506. The castle has not been remodelled and the original architectural form has been preserved almost completely intact until today.

The castle stands on a rectangular plot of land surrounded by moats with water that are fed by the Croisne. The small castle at the entrance with its two high towers and narrow embrasures for firearms, encloses the drawbridge. The chateau is built of red and black brick in a diamond pattern; stone is only used on the corners and window frames. On the west and southern walls, the bricks form a pattern of vertical rectangles, while others represent the wheel of a watermill (west), or form a symbolic pattern (south) that is found on ancient monuments.

Inside, between the entrance tower and the left corner tower, in the 16th-century building one finds the Guardroom, an old kitchen with crossed ogival arches that rest on a polygonal pillar.

Recently built (during the 19th and 20th centuries) the stone and timber annexes are quite delightful.

Views of the château of Lassay-sur-Croisne, surrounded by large moats, complete in its architecture modelled on medieval fortresses.

VALENÇAY

The name of Valençay probably derives from Valens, a Gallo-Roman owner of the estate which lies on a cliff overlooking the valley of the Nahon river. The original nucleus of buildings began to take form in the 3rd-4th centuries. A massive stone tower that was built between the 10th and the 11th centuries was the distant ancestor of the château we now see. The first real feudal castle was built at the beginning of the 13th century, perhaps by Gauthier, lord of Valençay. Inherited by the Chalon-Tonnerre family, it was restructured and enlarged. The Guardroom, an immense vaulted room, dates to this period. It is situated under the court of honour, access to which is from the subterranean areas of the castle through a corridor which probably connected the castle to the fortifications built to the north and west of the château. The other two sides were defended by the cliff and had no need of man-made defenses.

During the 15th century the seigniory of Valençay passed to the rich d'Etampes family, who demolished the old manor around 1540 and commissioned a sumptuous new residence. It is not certain who the architect called in by Jacques d'Etampes was. The names of both Philibert de l'Orme and Jean de l'Espine have been suggested but no documentary

Above, panoramic view of the château of Valençay.

Left, the château seen from the court of honour.

Talleyrand at Valençay

"Monsieur de Talleyrand, I want you to buy a fine estate, I want you to receive the members of the Diplomatic Corps, esteemed foreigners, I want people to want to come to your house and that being invited constitutes a reward for the ambassadors of the sovereigns who will content me..." With these words Napoleon Bonaparte had his minister of Foreign Affairs acquire Valençay, which was officially consigned in May of 1803 for the notable sum of 1,600,000 francs; Napoleon himself contributed to payment. It was an important decision and even today the château is still proudly associated with the name of Talleyrand. Indeed, every year altogether 100 days are dedicated to historic representations – an absolute record that makes Valençay the most lively of all the châteaux on the Loire. Visitors find themselves completely immersed in the atmosphere and settings of the early 19th century surrounded by characters in costume who represent Talleyrand's numerous retinue, the prince himself, the ladies in waiting to the Duchess of Dino, pages, soldiers and servants who bring to life the gardens and kitchens. As if by magic, history comes to life once more.

proof in favour of one or the other exists. Inspired by the neighbouring castle of Chambord, Jacques d'Etampes had the fine entrance pavilion, a sort of unusual tower, built. As at Chambord, the three superposed orders of pilasters have sculpted capitals. With its crown of machicolations, emphasized by an elaborate frieze, this fine castle is one of the masterpieces of the Renaissance. The corner towers and the main bodies of the building, highlighted by the fine Italian Gallery, also date to this period. At the beginning of the 17th century Dominique d'Etampes continued the construction, adding the west wing of the palace – overlooking the park – and the wing towards the east. The courtyard that opened on the valley was closed by an arcaded wall which connected the two wings of the building. The interiors were decorated by famous artists, including Jean Mosnier, who also worked in Cheverny and at the Palais du Luxembourg. The enthusiastic description of the château which Mad-emoiselle de Montpensier entrusted to her *Mémoires* after a sojourn at Valençay dates to 1653. In the second half of the 17th century, trials, family altercations and complex problems of succession led to the decline of the d'Etampes family and the property passed into the hands of the Chaumont de la Millière family. It was then bought in 1766 by Charles Legendre de Villemorien, who undertook new works of rebuilding. The east wing and the arcaded wall were demolished to open up the view over the city. Around 1770 the west wing was also transformed with the construction of the elegant South Tower at the end towards the valley. De Villemorien also infused new life into the economy of the estate, creating a silk factory and a smithy and increasing commercial activity.

His son, Comte de Lucay, who escaped the guillotine during the Revolution, ceded everything to Talleyrand in 1803 since he was no longer able to bear the burden of the costs involved in maintaining the

The splendid exterior of Valençay with its graceful façade.

property. Chronicles relate that Talleyrand, accompanied by Catherine Worlée, took three days to visit the entire estate: the château with its more than 100 rooms, the park of 150 hectares, the woods, the lands, the fields, the vineyards, 99 farms... for a total of 19,000 hectares, one of the largest feudal estates in France. As Napoleon had desired, for more than a quarter of a century the most important personalities of the time vied with each other to be received at Valençay by the great diplomat. Laying the blame for the undertaking of the war in Spain on Talleyrand, Napoleon, who intended to use Valençay as he pleased, ordered that it was to become the dwelling place of the Princes of Spain and their following for the six years they were in exile. When they arrived in May of 1808 the château proved insufficiently large to house their numerous following, who had to be lodged in the city, provoking considerable confusion.

To alleviate the gilded imprisonment of the princes, Napoleon ordered the unwilling Talleyrand, host-jailer, to construct the theatre near the orangerie: a real theatre in all senses, large enough to hold 150 spectators, with a stage as deep as the entire hall. The rich decoration of the interior is attributed to the Adam brothers, famous Scottish architects. It was inaugurated in 1810 and the most famous actors of the time appeared there. Some of the stage sets which were made in Paris have remained at the theatre which will soon be in use once more. It was also at the time of the sojourn of the Spanish princes that the park was completely surrounded by walls as a security measure. In 1806 Talleyrand had it turned into an English garden, setting up scenic routes and commissioning the architect Renard to build exotic constructions (the Turkish pavilion, the Cossack's house, the Egyptian temple, the Chinese bridge). The only building still extant is the one created for dances and other entertainment and which was later transformed into a hunting lodge. The

Above, the bedroom of King Ferdinand VII of Spain, exiled to Valençay (1808-1814) by Napoleon I.

Left, from the top, a view of the large salon furnished in empire style and the bathroom, with furnishings dated 1830.

imposing monumental staircase which joined the Duchess's garden to the vegetable garden has also disappeared. The park does, however, still contain the ice house which is as yet in working order.

On March 12, 1814, the Princes of Spain returned to their native land, and after the Congress of Vienna, the fall of the Empire and the return of the Bourbons, Talleyrand retired to Valençay with Dorothy, his nephew's wife and future Duchess of Dino, where he ordered considerable renovation to be carried out and cancelled all traces of the Spaniards. The château was reborn: sumptuous receptions and banquets marked by the culinary skill of the great Carême were given;

the smithy, the saw mills, the silk factory were once more put into working order; sheep raising was augmented by cross-breeding with merinos from England. Among the important persons who stayed in the château during the last years of Talleyrand's life were Duke Paul de Noailles, Princess de Lieven, Countess Tyskiewicz, Thiers, Balzac, Decazes, the Duke d'Orléans and, in 1834, George Sand. Talleyrand died in Paris on May 17, 1838 and was buried in Valençay as he had asked. The château and the estate passed to Louis de Talleyrand-Périgord named Duke of Valençay by Charles X. Since 1980 the château has been the property of a Departmental Association which administers it.

fine guards' room, and the bedroom of Maria Sobieska, queen of Poland.

During the summer, the rooms in the Gilded Pavilion are brought to life with performances depicting a typical day in the life of the castle.

St-Aignan-sur-Cher

Enclosed by narrow medieval streets overlooked by the church and château, St-Aignan is today a flourishing industrial town. For many years the stone fortress, built on a rise inside the town-walls, overlooked the roads crossing the area until, during the Renaissance, the Dukes of St-Aignan made it their luxurious residence. Between the end of the 15th and the beginning of the 16th centuries, a new château was built, in stone and brick, which has remained quite intact except for the western pavilion and the terrace overlooking the wooded Cher valley.

Above and left, the castle of Selles-sur-Cher.

Below, views of St-Aignan, with its château, reflected in the Cher.

Selles-sur-Cher

Originally, the castle was a fort built by Thibaut Le Tricheur over Merovingian foundations. Outside, the access bridge is flanked by two 17th-century stone and brick structures. At the far end of the park with its centuries old trees (including one of the oldest Lebanon cedars in Europe) stands the Gilded Pavilion. In the building to the right (the Béthune Pavilion) there is a

MONTRÉSOR

The castle overlooks the village of Montrésor on the axis of an ancient road, flanked by old houses that have been recently restored and from its vantage point it offers a marvellous view of the picturesque village and the Indrois valley.

At the beginning of the 11th century Fulk Nerra, a great builder and daring warrior, built a fortress on a rocky peak over the Indrois valley to block access to the plateau. In 1188 Philippe Auguste took possession of the castle and gave it to André de Chauvigny. In 1433 the castle served as prison for Georges de la Trémoille, a minister to King Charles VII. In 1493 the Basternay family turned it into a "salon" for the distinguished and intellectuals, and made the castle into a country home. The castle was restored in 1849 by Count Xavier Branicki, a Polish émigré who had accompanied Napoleon III to Constantinople and tried to raise a Polish regiment during the Crimean War. The castle can be reached via a 12th-century entrance, the same period as the corner towers. A wall, remains of the 11th century fortress, surrounds the castle. Within the walls stands the residential building that was erected in the 16th century with its mullioned windows, dormer windows and two towers with trap doors. The furnishings date from the era of Count Branicki. There are some interesting bas-relief wood sculptures depicting the battles between Jean III Sobieski, King of Poland, and the Ottomans.

Covering an area of scarcely a square kilometre and holding the record as the smallest village in Touraine, Montrésor is also one of the most beautiful villages in the entire region, if not indeed in all of France, with picturesque houses and fertile land where busy farms and cultivated fields nestle. One frequently comes across fascinating views and quite unique corners where the austere rural architecture succeeds in creating the illusion that time really has stood still here.

MONTPOUPON

This château rises in an isolated position between the valleys of the Indre and the Cher. It stands in a clearing at the conjunction of three small valleys which are traversed by five brooks. The road that connects Loches with Montrichard passes by the front of the building which has a particularly elegant aspect. The castle was begun in the 12th-13th centuries, as indicated by the oldest extant parts. The cylindrical keep, which widens slightly at the base, dates to this period. This massive structure is typically medieval in the limited number of narrow windows which appear only above a determined height, the widening of the summit and the stone bracket supports, and the presence of small windows and arrowslits on top.

A long wing for the apartments is set against the keep with its conical roof. The diversity of architectural concept identifies them as 15th and 16th century additions. True symmetry is lacking in the façade of the château, which is marked by a play of dark and light in which the masonry of the walls contrasts with the lighter colour of the corner stones and of the reinforcements at the windows. The left side terminates in a slender corner tower, with elongated windows with architraves, thus balancing the tower of the keep which rises behind it. The right side consists of a wing with lodgings characterized by faceted polygonal stonework. Dormers with triangular decorative superstructures are set into the high pitched slate roofs of the central block. The whole complex is surrounded by a low encircling wall which incorporates a cylindrical tower with a conical roof and a postern dating to the 16th century. Square in form, the latter has corner towers

Above and top right, two views of the château. Right, the saddlery with antique coaches and carriages and the trophy collection in the hunting room.

(the ones on the façade are set on jutting corbels) between which is the portal, a window, and a dormer. The gate leads to the court of honour with the castle well. The building was originally used by gentlemen when they went hunting and for a long time it belonged to the De Prie family, which included Louise de Prie, governess of the French heirs to the throne. Today the manor belongs to the family of De la Motte St-Pierre.

69

LOCHES

The history of the château of Loches is intimately tied to the history of France as far back as the 10th century. At that time a wooden tower for defense rose on the highest point of a rocky plateau. It was connected to the surrounding countryside by tunnels excavated in the rock. At the beginning of that century the feudal domain belonged to Fulk I the Red, Count of Anjou, whose descendant Fulk Nerra created one of the first square forts in stone here.

Fulk Nerra made a name for himself in French history as a warrior, and the birth of military architecture in stone owes a great deal to him. He was a great builder of defensive works and realized several dozen forts based on new dictates which at the time made them impregnable. The tower at Loches, with a base measuring 25 by 15 metres, was built between 1005 and 1070. Its walls, over 38 metres in height and between two and three metres thick, are still pierced by holes for the scaffolding that was erected when it was built as well as holes for the suspension of the battlement platforms, wooden structures which were suspended in the

Above, the façade of the royal apartments. Left, Joan of Arc Meeting Charles VII at Loches, by Alexandre Millin du Perreux (1764-1843).
Right, a view of the fortress with the large keep.

void and from which projectiles were hurled at the attackers. The three floors inside had chimneys whose vents can be seen from the outside. In 1040 Nerra died at Loches, where he was buried, and his successor Geoffroi Martel of Anjou succeeded in defeating the Counts of Blois at St-Martin-le-Beau. The house of Anjou thus came into possession of Loches – where other defenses were built towards the south – and the surrounding territory, until the last of the Fulks married the daughter of the Duke of Normandy, King of England. Their son, Henry Plantagenet, also became King of England, in 1154. But it was not long before disagreements arose between him and Philippe Auguste, King of France, who took a large part of their dominions from the Plantagenets. When Henry II Plantagenet died, his son Richard the Lion-Heart went to the Holy Land for the Third Crusade. Upon his return he fell prisoner to emperor Henry VI of Austria and Philippe Auguste was able to obtain various territories including Loches from Richard's brother, John Lackland. Free once more, Richard the Lion-Heart recaptured Loches in 1195 after only three hours of fighting. His legitimate heir, Arthur, was assassinated by John Lackland against whom Philippe Auguste of France moved once more, taking Loches in 1205 after a year-long siege. The Crown of France, which has owned the castle since then, incremented the defenses adding the *Vieux Logis* to the north, with a tower and a sentinel's walk, in the 13th century. In June 1429, after

the taking of Orléans, Joan of Arc arrived here to convince Charles VII to move on Reims and be crowned king. And it was this same Charles VII who in 1444 had Agnès Sorel, the lovely lady-in-waiting who became the first mistress of a king in the history of France, stay in one of the towers here. During the 15th century the Kings of France completed the *Vieux Logis* with new dwelling constructions, the New Tower and the Martelet. The Logis Royaux thus was eventually comprised of a 13th-century tower and a wall, a block of constructions with a 14th-century guard tower, and a hunting pavilion dating to the 15th century, contemporary with still another bastion in which passageways for various streets were opened (Porte des Cordeliers, tower of St Anthony). The new wing contains the chapel of Anne de Bretagne, wife first of Charles VIII and then of Louis XII. When she was only 23, Anne had already suffered the loss of her parents, her husband and four children. The queen was fond of retiring into a small room she had had prepared in Loches, where she could pray. Silver Breton ermines were sculpted on the walls on a blue ground, and an altar and a fireplace decorated the corners of the room.

Part of the castle of Loches was used as a prison and many famous personages occupied the cells from the 15th century on. In 1469 Cardinal de la Balue was imprisoned in the circular tower. He had conspired against King Louis XI, causing him to be taken prisoner by Charles the Bold. Still today it is

Agnès Sorel

AGNES SOREL

Known as the lady of Beauté (both for her beauty as well as for the estate of Beauté-en-Champagne given to her by the king), Agnès was only twenty when Charles, in his forties, fell in love with her. Agnès took an interest in the affairs of court and loved to surround herself with luxury, so that the king often gave her jewels and rare oriental products. Despite this she was very devout and was a benefactress of the local church of Notre-Dame in Loches, today known as St-Ours. This church had been built on the land belonging to the fort between the 11th and 12th centuries. Palmettes, human figures, monsters and animals of obvious Romanesque origin decorate the portal, above which is an "Adoration of the Magi". The interior dates in part to the 11th century and in part to the 14th and 15th centuries. Agnes died in 1450, at only 28 years of age, apparently due to complications arising from a difficult pregnancy. Even so rumours were that she had been poisoned by the dauphin who had tried to seduce her, forcing her to leave Chinon for Loches. Agnès requested that she be buried in the church she had endowed and to which she left an inheritance of 2,000 gold scudi. The sculpted tombstone there is a copy of the alabaster original. It shows the lady of Beauté with her hands joined, watched over by two small angels and with two lambs at her feet.

Above, a portrait of Agnès Sorel, by Jean Fouquet, and a detail of her tomb in the Romanesque church of St-Ours (below).

remembered that the cardinal was enclosed in a cage which he himself, the height of irony, had invented and which was known as the "little girl" because it was so small (1.50x1.75 m). Suspended beams and pulleys permitted the cage to be suspended several metres above the ground at night to avoid the possibility of flight.

Ludovico Sforza, known as il Moro, Duke of Milan, was also detained in the Martelet. This refined scholar had been taken prisoner at the battle of Novara and after an initial period in Bourges he was confined to Loches. Because of his rank, Louis XII permitted him to have various comforts such as the company of a court jester and of teachers and the use of furniture and a fireplace. He himself decorated the walls and barrel vault of the cell with a helmet, snakes, stars and various mottos (including "He who is not content"). For eight years, up to 1508, il Moro remained closed in this room. It is said that as soon as he was freed, he died at the sight of the light and open air.

In the dungeons of the castle, the torture chamber – created in the middle of the 15th century by Charles VII – still preserves the bar with rings which imprisoned the ankles of the prisoners.

The keep: right, the staircase that led to the secret prison of Cardinal La Balue (advisor to Louis XI who betrayed the king to Charles the Bold); below, the torture chamber.

CHAUMONT

The château of Chaumont (from "Chauve Mont" or Bald Hill, then changed into "Chaud Mont" or Hot Hill) stands on a rise beside the river Loire, in the midst of a dense wood of tall trees.

As early as the Middle Ages a castle already stood here. The first owner of Chaumont was Gelduin, who was saved from having to leave the castle to his daughter Claire when a son, Geoffroi, was born to him late in life. The boy's effeminate beauty earned him the nickname of "little girl" and despite his legendary physical resistance, Geoffroi never married and was for a long time considered a hermaphrodite. The first castle made of wood was destroyed, only to be reconstructed and then destroyed once more in 1465, when Louis XI used this as a means of punishing Pierre d'Amboise – the owner at the time – for having sided with the League of the Common Weal. Immediately after its demolition, Pierre had work begun on the present castle, which was initially meant for military use and was not nearly as comfortable as it seems now. Italian Renaissance influences which lighten the austere west wing – the oldest – are evident. The windows were added later.

The other wings are more recent and reveal a more generalized Renaissance character. Construction continued for three generations. Pierre was followed by his son Charles, the first of 17 brothers, and his grandson Charles II. The reliefs at the entrance refer to Charles II who succeeded in completing the château. Two entwined C's sculpted on the circular towers which flank the drawbridge refer to him and his wife Catherine. The French coat of arms with the initials of Louis XII and his wife Anne de Bretagne is set over the entrance door, while the towers bear the coats of arms of Charles II and his uncle Georges I, Cardinal of Amboise.

In 1560, after the death of Henry II, Catherine de' Medici bought the château. A beautiful room with tapestries is in fact attributed to her. In the brief period of her occupation another Florentine was also occasionally present in Chaumont, Cosimo Ruggieri, who had come to France together with the queen. Officially an astrologer based in the Breton Abbey of St-Mahé, he may really have been a charlatan or an occultist, although some say he was a true scholar. One of his laboratories and observatories, where Ruggieri often met with the queen, can

*Above, the entrance to the château; right,
the court of honour.*

This splendid and elegant château offers many interesting aspects to its visitors. A grand court with a graceful antique well welcomes them. Around the castle, just as worthy of our attention and admiration, is a large park where every year from mid June to mid October the spectacular International Garden Festival is held. Arriving from all over the world, about twenty artists and landscape artists participate, creating stupendous thematic gardens on an area of land that is made available to them. And they remain until the autumn - always a magnificent moment in the Loire Valley when the harmonious beauty of the area seems to reach its greatest splendour.

Jacques le Ray. Under Le Ray, during the 18th century, the Italian Nini created a factory of fine ceramics (some of the medallions are now on exhibit in the castle) in the nearby annexes. Using the clay from the Loire, Nini produced many portraits of notables which became very popular and made Le Ray a rich man. During the Empire the famous Madame de Staël, whom Napoleon had enjoined to live at least 40 leagues from Paris, moved to the château where she surrounded herself with sympathizers.

In the 19th century the north wing was totally demolished so as to provide a panorama of the Loire and the surrounding park. The Broglie family also had the stables, a unique conical angular construction, built. In 1938 the State bought the castle. Restored and furnished, it has been open to the public since then.

Left, a portrait of Catherine de' Medici.

Facing page, above, the bedroom that belonged to Catherine de' Medici's astrologer, Cosimo Ruggieri; below, the neo-Gothic fireplace built by the Broglie family in the 19th century; and the spiral staircase dating from the Gothic period.

Below, Catherine de' Medici's bedroom.

be reached through one of the towers. Some tales tell of how when the moon was full Ruggieri could see the king and his children in a magic mirror, revealing how many years they would live and how many years they would reign according to the number of revolutions the image made on the surface of the enchanted object. In any case, Ruggieri was involved in various intrigues, both political and behind-the-scenes, prejudicial to the queen herself in whose palaces he had numerous observers. One of these conspiracies led to his detention in jail while his complices ended up on the gallows. His temporary rehabilitation did not hinder him from returning to prison accused of witchcraft against Henry IV.

The château of Chaumont was also offered by Catherine to the lovely Diane de Poitiers, formerly Henry II's mistress, in exchange for the larger building of Chenonceau. Actually Diane did live for a short while at Chaumont: her room – which can still be seen – and the sculpted coats of arms, identifiable by a horn, a bow and a quiver with her initials, date to this period. Thereafter the castle passed to the Viscount of Turenne d'Auvergne, the Duc de St-Aignan Charles de Beauvillier, and to

77

Gué-Péan

A few kilometres from Pontlevoy, in Loir-et-Cher, stands the château of Gué-Péan. Used as a hunting lodge, the complex dates to the 14th and 15th centuries.

The ground plan is square and it now has a gateway at the centre of the encircling walls. Two low semi-cylindrical towers, with terraces on top, flank the entrance. Three blocks of buildings arranged in a U pattern face onto the immense court of honour. The principal block, at the back of the courtyard, is flanked by cylindrical towers with conical roofs. The rather low façade has numerous windows which mitigate the severe aspect of the castle and admit light. Elegant dormers with superstructures decorate the roof. The block on the left, which also has dormers, is in communication with a cylindrical tower that reinforces the front corner of the walls. The tower widens near the top, with sustaining brackets, and has a helmet-shaped dome with a small lantern, rather like the towers of the châteaux of Serrant and Valençay.

Throughout the centuries numerous kings (Francis I, Henry II, Henry III) and famous men (La Fayette, Balzac) stayed in the elegant Renaissance apartments. Today the rooms of the château, which is owned by the Marquis of Keguelin, are open to the public. Of particular interest are the guardroom, the chapel, the hall and the library. The rooms are furnished with fireplaces, artistic items and antique furniture in Louis

From the top, a view of the austere château of Gué-Péan, the hall, furnished in Louis XV style, with the monumental fireplace by Germain Pilon, and the large hall with 18th-century furniture.

XV and Louis XVI style, with tapestries and paintings (including works by A. del Sarto, J.L. David, H. Rigaud, G. Reni, J.H. Fragonard), while the library contains a valuable collection of historical documents.

CHANTELOUP

The highly original pagoda of Chanteloup, not far from Amboise, is all that remains of the château of Chanteloup, the "little Versailles" built by the Duke of Choiseul, a minister of Louis XV, and where he was forced to live by the king after his fall from grace and subsequent removal from court in December 1770. In 1775, the duke directed his architect, Le Camus, to build the striking pagoda in homage to the loyalty of his friends. 44 metres high, this singular obelisk combines 18th century French style with the typical features of Chinese monuments, in a completely unique union. Restored in 1910 by the architect René-Edouard André, today it hosts a permanent exhibition illustrating the historical events of the great château of Chanteloup, destroyed in 1823, and its charming gardens.

MONTRICHARD

The town of Montrichard, with its unmistakeable white houses, faces the river Cher, overlooked by the powerful bulk of the château. The original nucleus was a square stone bastion, built in 1120 by Hugo I d'Amboise, resembling the one at Loches. In the following centuries, starting with the

restoration works requested by Richard Lion-Heart, fortified walls, cylindrical towers, a drawbridge and, finally, the rooms of the main residence were added, thus transforming Montrichard into a fully-fledged and elegant château.

Above, the lofty pagoda the last and unusual remaining element of what was once the castle of Chanteloup. Left, the castle of Montrichard, overlooking the town.

Chenonceau

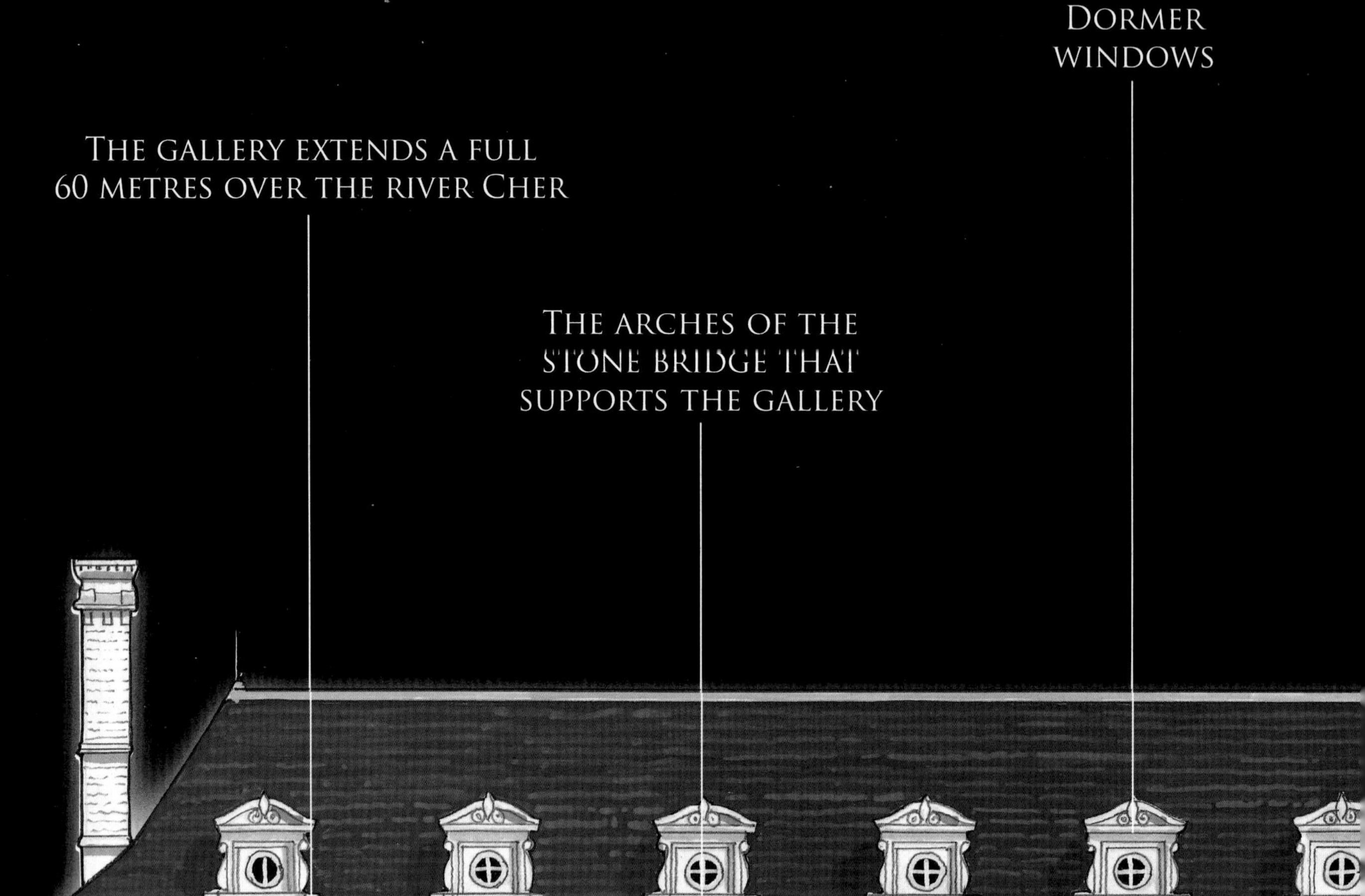

DORMER
WINDOWS

THE GALLERY EXTENDS A FULL
60 METRES OVER THE RIVER CHER

THE ARCHES OF THE
STONE BRIDGE THAT
SUPPORTS THE GALLERY

THE SECOND FLOOR OF
THE GALLERY, WHICH
HOUSED THE BALLROOM

THE MAIN BODY OF THE
CHATEAU WITH THE ROOM
OF DIANE DE POITIERS AND
THE GREEN ROOM

GOTHIC
CHAPEL

CHENONCEAU

In 1243 the territory on which the château of Chenonceau is built belonged to the house of Marques, originally from Auvergne. A defensive fortress surrounded by moats and joined to the banks of the river Cher with a swing bridge and a mill, stood on the site of the elegant Renaissance building now to be seen. During Charles VI's reign the owner of the fort, Jean Marques, granted asylum to an English garrison. As a result the king had the defenses dismantled but salvaged the building and left the lands to the Marques. The family was always in debt and, as time passed, was

*The château as it stretches along the banks of the Cher
with Catherine de' Medici's beautiful gardens.*

forced to sell almost all its lands to Thomas Bohier, Intendent of Finance for Normandy. In the end he also bought the small fortress in 1512, but as it did not correspond to the latest Renaissance mode, Bohier decided to construct a new castle and tore down the one that was already standing. The only remaining medieval part is the tower of the keep, set in front of the castle which was mostly rebuilt.

A rectangular building with corner towers, erected around an internal vestibule with ogee vaulting, was built on what remained of the mill. There were four rooms on the ground floor, while a straight staircase (the spiral staircase was generally abandoned in the early 16th century) led to the first floor where there were four more rooms. The high costs of the construction seem to explain the motto the Bohiers had sculpted together with their initials T.B.K. "S'il vient a point, me souviendra" (If the castle is finished, it will preserve my memory).

Building activity, which Catherine Bohier, Thomas's wife, had overseen in the absence of her husband, was finished in 1521, when cardinal Bohier, archbishop of Bourges, consecrated the château chapel. In 1524 Thomas Bohier died in Italy in the service of the king, and two years later his wife also died.

Inherited by their son Antoine, the castle was soon confiscated by Francis I in repayment of various deficits for which Thomas was held responsible. Some say it was expropriated in 1533 because the king wanted to come into possession of this splendid building set in the midst of an estate abounding in game. And Francis I did go to Chenonceau, sometimes accompanied by a small group of close friends: Queen Eleanor, his son Henry, Catherine de' Medici, his mistress Anne de Pisseleu lady of Heuilly and Diane de St-Vallier de Poitiers, his son's mistress. The castle was the scene of hunts on horseback, fêtes, suppers and intellectual activi-

In the annex, outside the château, is a small Wax Museum. The scenes reproduced include the most famous inhabitants of Chenonceau and the most outstanding episodes in its history. Catherine Bohier is shown with a minstrel, Diane de Poitiers is in the woods during a hunt and with Henry II, Madame Dupin is shown receiving Rousseau and Voltaire and, in an other episode, posing for the painter Nattier. There is also a reconstruction of the military hospital set up in 1914.

The Wax Museum: King Henry II with his favourite, Diane de Poitiers.

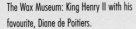

ties, in accordance with the ideals of the period. Many stories, which were frequently slanderous, circulated regarding Diane de Poitiers. Some said that she had conceded her favours to Henry II's father, Francis I, so that he would intercede in favour of her father; others said that Francis I had asked her to put some sense into the head of his son Henry who was still very immature, and that she had answered that she would make him her lover. Whatever the truth, Diane had great influence over Henry II and once on the throne, in 1547, even though he was married to Catherine de' Medici, he continued to shower her with gifts. Even though he was 19 years younger than Diane, the new King of France used the crescent moon (symbol of the goddess Diana) as his emblem and dressed in the colours his mistress preferred, black and white. It was not long before the château of Chenonceau was also donated to

Diane de Poitiers, despite the numerous legal cavils which decreed the building to be the property of the Crown and therefore inalienable. Together with the jewels of the Crown, Henry II assigned part of the royal fiscal revenue to his mistress. With this conspicuous sum at her disposal, Diane de Poitiers began the works of improvement including the layout of the garden with flowers, fruits and vegetables which at the

The façade seen from the gardens of Diane de Poitiers.

time were considered exotic, such as melons and artichokes. She also had soundings taken of the bottom of the Cher for the construction of a masonry bridge, designed by Philibert Delorme and soon built.

Despite the passing of time, Diane's beauty remained unchanged, as witnessed by the painting which shows her nude next to a stag. It is said that her secret was in diving into cold water as soon as she got up, riding and walking and then going back to bed until noon. However, in 1559, as Nostradamus had predicted, Henry II died after having been seriously wounded in one eye by a spear during a tournament. The queen, Catherine de' Medici, free to act as she pleased, began to avenge herself on the lovely Diane and asked her to return the Crown jewels and the castle. After attempts at resistence, Diane was forced to give in and withdrew to the château of Anet where she stayed until she died at 66 years of age. Once she had Chenonceau, Catherine organized a great celebration in honour of her son Francis II and his wife, Mary Stuart. For these celebrations Primaticcio prepared a grandiose ornamental apparatus consisting of columns, statues, fountains, triumphal arches and obelisks, while a battery of 30 cannons was set up to fire salutes from the courtyard. New gardens, together with the annexes, were finished in 1568 and

The portrait of Louis XIV by Hyacinthe Rigaud (1659-1743).

Facing page, above left, the fireplace by Jean Goujon in Diane de Poitiers's bedroom; above right, Primaticcio (1504-1570), Diane de Poitiers portrayed as a huntress. Below, the Louis XIV salon with the fireplace decorated with the salamander and the ermine, emblems of Francis I and Claude of France.

Catherine de'Medici's bedroom.

inaugurated with a great fête together with the ratification of the peace of Amboise. Another unforgettable celebration was held in 1577 when Henry II returned from Poland for the succession of Charles IX. For the occasion the novel device invented by Henry for his festivities at Plessis-lès-Tours was used: the women disguised themselves as men and vice versa. Henry himself wore a gown of pink and silver brocade, with violets and diamonds in his hair and pearls at his neck. The depth of his decollete made Pierre de l'Estoile say that "it was difficult to tell at a glance if it was a king-woman or a queen-man". In 1580 the architect Androuet du Cerceau began work on a new wing that stretched across the bridge on the Cher. The new building had two floors and its long façades were ably enlivened with windows, projections and dormer windows.

The upper floor was to be used as a ball room and was decorated like the rest of the château with rich furnishings. The sumptuous festivals inspired by antiquity and myths,

in which the ladies of the court often appeared half naked (hoping to gather useful private information to pass on to Catherine), ended when in 1589 the queen mother died in Blois. Her testament entrusted the château of Chenonceau to Louise de Vaudémont, wife of her son Henry III. A few months later – in August of 1589 – Henry was killed by Jacques Clément. It is said that before he drew his last breath the king dictated a letter for his wife in which he said: "My beloved, I hope to be well: pray God for me and do not move from there". These words may have induced the queen to stay in the palace until she died. All bright furnishings were done away with and were replaced by black drapes and attributes of death. In response to her desire for prayer the Ursuline nuns came to live in the palace. She dressed in white – the colour of royal mourning according to an ancient tradition – ever after until 1601 when the "White Dame" died. The château was inherited by Françoise de Mercoeur, wife of César, Duke of Vendôme.

From then on the Kings of France stopped there only rarely. The last French sovereign to stay in Chenonceau was Louis XIV in 1650.

The state of neglect the Vendômes and the Bourbon-Condés had left the building in was briefly interrupted when one wing was used as a Capucine monastery. A drawbridge, meant to isolate the monks from the rest of the world, remains from this period.

In 1733 the Duke of Bourbon sold the castle to Claude Dupin, a wealthy financier. His wife, a lover of art, the sciences, literature and theatre, created a bourgeois salon at Chenonceau which included the most famous names of the time. Fontenelle, Buffon, Montesquieu, Mably, Marivaux, Voltaire, Condillac, Madame de Tency and Madame du Deffand often stayed in the castle. Jean Jacques Rousseau became Madame Dupin's secretary and tutor for her daughter. He wrote: "One passed the time well in that lovely place and one ate well: I became as fat as a friar. We made music and recited plays. I composed an opera in verse entitled *L'Allée de Sylvie* after the name of a boulevard in the park which skirts the Cher". In fact Madame Dupin had set up a small theatre for the presentation of plays as well as a laboratory for the study of physics. The rooms of the preexisting apartments had also been rebuilt and made more comfortable.

In 1782 the château came to be lived in all year round by its learned owner, who was so respected and loved by the local population that Chenonceau came through the Revolution unharmed. Abbot Lecomte, the local curate, intervened against the most ardent revolutionaries, telling

The room known as the chamber "of the five queens."

Above, the interior of the gallery that boldly projects over the Cher, designed by Philibert Delorme.

Left, The Three Graces by Carl van Loo (1705-1765).

them: "There is only one bridge between Montrichard and Bléré, and you want to tear it down! You are the enemies of the common good!" Madame Dupin was thus able to live in her castle until 1799 when she died at the age of 93 and was buried in the park. Abandoned, the château was sold in 1864 by the heirs to Madame Pelouze, who started to restore the castle to its appearance before Catherine de' Medici's transformations. Although some of the windows were eliminated, together with the caryatids on the façade, the monumental wing on the Cher was left untouched. The Pelouzes soon fell into debt and in 1888 the château was confiscated by the Land Trust which sold it to Henri Menier, one of the wealthiest industrialists of the time. His brother, and then his heirs, are still the owners of Chenonceau. One of the most meritorious acts in the history of the castle was when Gaston Menier, senator of Seine-et-Marne, transformed the building in 1914 into a temporary hospital where more than two thousand wounded were recovered up to the end of World War I. After having played an important role in the

crossing of the partisan forces in the last war, the château with its bridge over the Cher has been completely restored and can be visited. The entrance to the estate leads through a long avenue lined with age-old trees to a vast open space on the left of which are the gardens laid out by Diane de Poitiers. In the corner of the court of honour, surrounded by the waters of the river, is the cylindrical tower which, partly rebuilt, dates back to medieval times. A drawbridge communicates with the ground floor of the castle where 16th-century tapestries are exhibited in the guardroom. Sculpture in Carrara marble, including a *Virgin and Child*, are to be found in the chapel. In addition to the green room and Diane de Poitiers' room, one can visit the gallery with paintings by Rubens, Primaticcio, Van Loo, Mignard and Nattier. A straight staircase leads to the first floor with the room of Gabrielle d'Estrées, the royal chamber (or "of the five queens"), Catherine de' Medici's room and that of Charles de Vendôme. The original cooking area and a unique, ingenious spit are still to be found in the kitchen.

CLOS-LUCÉ

In 1214 Sulpice III, of the house of Amboise, gave the religious community of Moncé the land on which the château of Clos-Lucé was to be built. The building in pink brick and white stone was constructed at the time of Louis XI on the foundations of an earlier construction dating to the Gallo-Roman period. It was then bought by Etienne le Loup, an enterprising scullion boy in the kitchens of the royal castle of Plessis-lès-Tours, who in a lightning career had become one of Louis XI's favoured counselors. At the time, despite the gardens, the large dovecote in brick (still to be seen) and its vineyards, the château of Clos-Lucé was a fortified dwelling with a lookout tower which is still in perfect condition, narrow windows, a postern and a drawbridge, traces of which are still visible next to the entrance. When Etienne le Loup fell into disgrace, the château was bought on the 2nd of July, 1490, for 3,500 gold scudi by Charles VIII and, since it was now a royal residence, was renovated by skilled artisans, stone cutters and painters called in from Naples. The chapel built in tufa for Queen Anne de Bretagne dates to this period. A host of famous figures lived in the castle at one time or another: the young Duke of Angoulême, the future Francis I, his sister Margaret of Navarre, who probably began to write her collection of short stories (*Heptameron*) here, Louise of Savoy when she was regent, Leonardo da Vinci, as well as other notable figures of history including the favorite Babou de la Bourdaisière, the captain of Henry III's guards, Michel du Gast who participated in the assassination of the Duke of Guise, St Francis of Paola and Henry III. The château then passed into the hands of the d'Amboise family who kept it from being destroyed at the time of the French Revolution. It has now belonged to the St-Bris family for several generations. In 1955 Hubert St-Bris decided to restore the castle to what it looked like when Leonardo da Vinci, the most famous of its many guests, lived there. The complex restoration was entrusted to the architect of the Monuments Historiques, Bernard Vitry, and the work to specialized craftsmen of the Beaux-Arts. Thanks to them Leonardo's kitchen (the Old Guardroom), the Council room and the subterranean chambers where Leonardo's splendid machines can be seen, the room of Margaret of Navarre and the room of Leonardo, are gradually returning to their original appearance.

Facing page, a view of the château and, left, the "great hall" with 15th-century furnishings used by Leonardo da Vinci.

Below, Leonardo da Vinci's kitchen and the bed where he died on 2 May 1519.

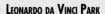

Leonardo da Vinci Park

In the autumn of 1516, on the invitation of Francis I, Leonardo left Italy, accompanied by a servant and his pupil Francesco Melzi. He reached France after a long journey on muleback, bringing with him *La Gioconda, St. John the Baptist* and *St. Anne.* In exchange for the château of Clos-Lucé (which was practically next to the palace at Amboise and at the time was called Cloux) and an annuity of 700 gold scudi, the king asked nothing of Leonardo but the pleasure of his conversation. The artist however amply repaid the king by organizing memorable fêtes and fantastic performances, such as on 17 June 1518, when Galeazzo Visconti was present and of which he left a detailed description. The admiration and love of the court did not, however, distract Leonardo from his studies and drawings, which he loved more than anything else. Despite the infirmity which is said to have involved his right hand, he obstinately dedicated himself to geometry, architecture, city planning and water works. A large number of manuscripts produced after October of 1517 testify to the fervid activity of this period. These include a sheet of the Codex Atlanticus with the annotation "Palazzo di Cloux d'Amboise, il 24 giugno 1518". Probably from this period are the projects for the castle of Romorantin, those for the draining of the Sologne and those for houses which could be taken apart and which were designed specifically for the court, which was always moving from one place to another. Many drawings preserved in the Royal Library of Windsor Castle (heads of old men, sketches for fêtes and carousels and drawings of the château of Amboise seen from one of the windows of Clos-Lucé) undoubtedly date to this period. In his will of April 23, 1519, written by the court notary, Leonardo left all his books, his drawings and the instruments relative to the art of painting to Francesco Melzi; to his servant Battista and to Salay he left, in equal parts, the land he owned in Milan; to Mathurine, the maid, a dress of black wool lined with fur, a length of wool and ducats. He died in the château on May 2, 1519, at the age of 67, and was buried in Amboise, in the royal cloister of St-Florentin. When the cloister was destroyed, his mortal remains were transferred to the

Chapel of St-Hubert in the château of Amboise. The chateau has recently created an unusual and original Leonardo da Vinci Park dedicated to the Tuscan genius, with three thematic areas, reconstructions of 40 of his machines, recordings in which the 'voice' of Leonardo speaks of his ideas and notions, a video on his life, actors in period costume, drawings, paintings and scenes of great historic and scientific interest.

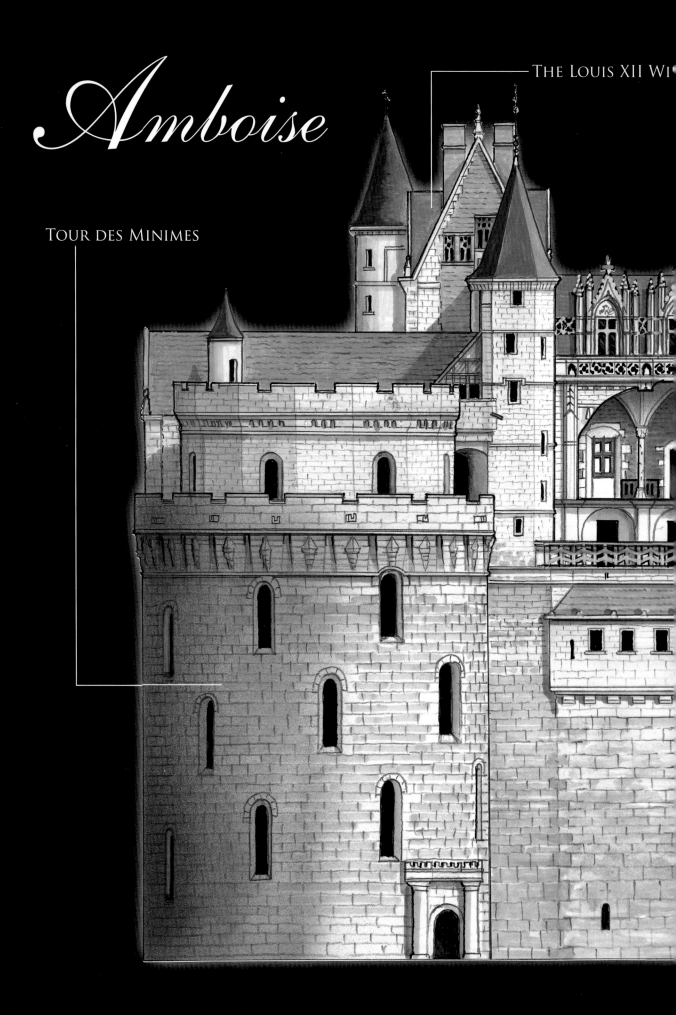

Amboise

TOUR DES MINIMES

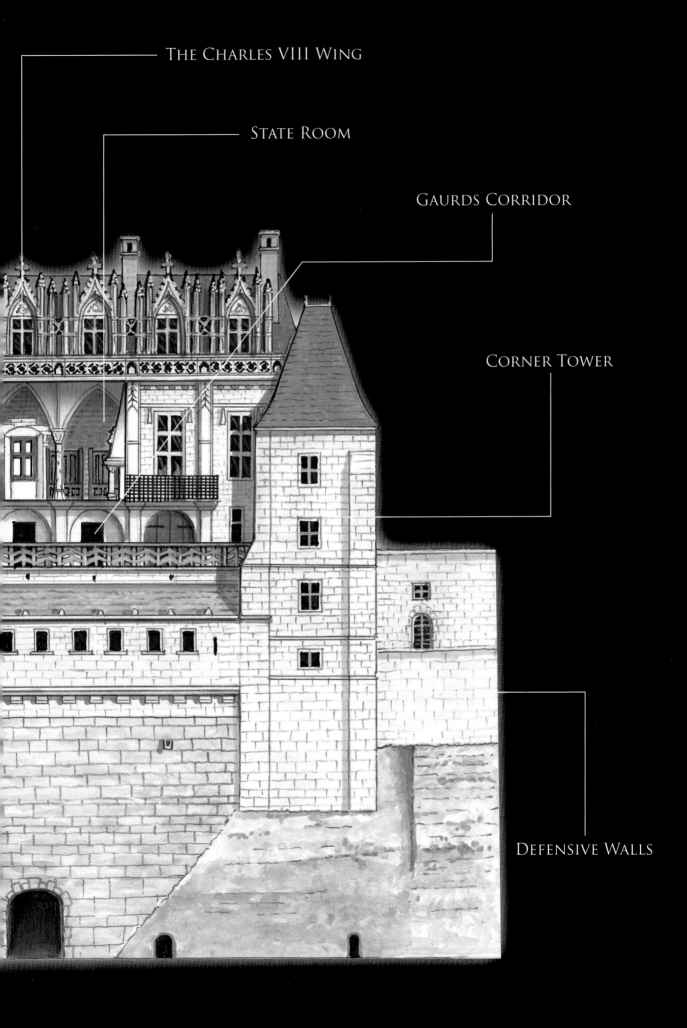

THE CHARLES VIII WING

STATE ROOM

GAURDS CORRIDOR

CORNER TOWER

DEFENSIVE WALLS

Aerial view of the castle on the banks of the Loire.

The château seen from the river.

This picturesque town, in its delightful setting on the banks of the Loire, is distinguished by its majesty and a lively sense of history. Residence of French Kings between the 15th and 16th centuries, it was the birthplace of Charles VIII who also died there at the early age of 28 (in 1498); it was also home to Leonardo da Vinci during the last three years of his life which ended in 1519. Other highlights at Amboise include the **Clos-Lucé**; the **Church of St-Denis** (12th century with additions and changes made in the 15th-16th centuries); the **Hôtel de Ville** (16th-century); and the **Church of St-Florentin** (15th-century).

AMBOISE

Clovis I, King of the Franks, and Alaric II, King of the Visigoths, met on the Ile St-Jean, in the centre of the Loire, below the present castle. Devastated by the Normans more than once, Amboise was first part of the possessions of the Counts of Anjou and then belonged to the famous house of Amboise-Chaumont until 1422, when it was inherited by Louis, Viscount of Thouars. Found guilty of plotting against the king, the owner of the château of Amboise was deprived of his lands.

From 1431 on, the castle belonged to the Crown. The "chastel d'Amboise" was no longer solely a fortress, but a royal residence and the city was benefited by the concession of receiving payment of the franchise. One of the great events in the reign of King Louis XI was the creation at Amboise of the Order of St- Michael on the first of August in 1469. That day the king gathered together fifteen of his most powerful barons in the chapel of St-Michael to acquaint them with the statute of this order of knighthood, whose foundation was of specifically political significance. The order of St-Michael represented the bond that tied the great lords and landed proprieters to the royal Crown. That day Amboise was the scene of a grand ceremony which remained in the annals of the kingdom.

Queen Charlotte, who died there in 1483, was always surrounded by a large court as befitted her rank. She had almost 150 persons in her following and service.

The apartments had been decorated and furnished in an effort to make her abode as pleasing as possible. The serene life he had lived there when he was young explains why the new King Charles VIII was so attached to the château where he had been born and raised. It was in the Place du Carroir at Amboise that the young 13-year old dauphin received Margaret of Austria, granddaughter of Charles the Bold, whom his father had decided to give him as wife. Margaret was only three years old when she was engaged to Charles VIII and lived in the château of Amboise until 1492 when she had to return to Flanders with a heavy heart, renouncing her place to Anne de Bretagne whom Charles VIII had married on December 6, 1491. Great construction works were undertaken at this time, financed by the income from taxes. The plans were magnificent: "he wants to turn the castle into a city" exclaimed the Florentine ambassador when he saw the projects late in 1493. The area of the building had to be considerably enlarged. A large trapezoid divided into three courtyards took the place of the old Medieval fortress.

The two spiral turrets, the Minimes tower and the Hurtault tower, were important architectural innovations. As for the decoration, it was initially of French inspiration but later profited from the collaboration of Flemish artists and, after the return of the Italian expedition of 1495, of Italian artists. The furnishings were luxurious: Flemish and French tapestries, Damask curtains and Turkish carpets.

The imposing construction works which aimed at transforming the antique "oppidum" and the old fortress of the Counts of Anjou into an abode worthy of the Crown of France were interrupted

Left, Gustave Noël, The Royal Château, the King's Residence (c. 1840).

A view of the château.

Above, the Cupbearer's Room and, right, the bedroom of Henry II.

by a mortal accident that befell the king in Amboise on April 7, 1498. While Charles was accompanying the queen in the Haquelebac gallery on his way to a ball game, it is said, he hit his forehead on a low door and died a few hours later. His successor was the Duke of Orléans who took the name of Louis XII, but the château of his choice was Blois, where much work was done during his reign and where he went to live with Anne de Bretagne, widow of Charles VIII, whom he married on January 8, 1499.

In 1500-1501 work was resumed and great quantities of stone were brought in to complete the buildings, particularly the Hurtault tower, and to create the gardens on the terraces above the Loire. With the accession of Francis I the châ-

Above, the hall of the States; left, the Récamier style bed in the bedroom of Louis Philip.

Facing page, a view of the Louis Philip hall.

teau once more shone. From 1515 to 1518 the king sojourned in what he called "that sumptuous château" when he came to the banks of the Loire, and after Marignano he returned to Amboise in 1516. Queen Claude gave birth to her three children here.

During the reign of Henry II, Catherine de' Medici, who loved Amboise, lived there with the children of the royal house. The château was later abandoned by the court of Valois and if the young King Francis II and his wife Mary Stuart, the queen mother, children, servants and following all arrived there on February 22, 1560 at the beginning of the new reign, this was because they had to flee from Blois and the conspiracy plotted by Condé which broke out at the beginning of the month.

The famous conspiracy of Amboise was severely repressed and three years later, on May 19, 1563, the queen mother, Catherine de' Medici, and the Prince de Condé stipulated the treaty which put an end to the first religious uprisings and allowed freedom of worship to the Protestant aristocracy.

After these extraordinary events, the château of Amboise ceased to be a royal residence even though Louis XIII occasionally lived here. In 1627 it became part of the property of Gaston d'Orléans and in 1660 returned to the Crown of France. But by that time the château was no longer really inhabitable, for it had in part been demolished. In 1762 the Duke of Choiseul bought the château, the baronage and the territory of Amboise which his heirs sold in 1786 to the Duke of Penthièvre. During the Revolution the château was confiscated and once more despoiled. Army barracks were installed and a button factory was set up between the logis des Sept-Vertus and the chapel of St-Hubert.

But it was later, under the First Empire, that Amboise was most seriously mutilated and even systematically demolished by the

member of parliament Roger-Ducos, who as senator was a beneficiary of the settlement of Orléans and was assigned the château of Amboise as his residence. Lacking the means to maintain it, the only solution he found was that of largely destroying it. In 1815 it was restored to the heiress, the Duchess of Orléans.

When the Duchess of Orléans died in 1821, her son, the future King Louis Philip, inherited the château and the property of Amboise. Louis Philip acquired 46 houses and barracks which surrounded the château in rue des Minimes and at Porte Hurtault and had them torn down, freeing the towers and the encircling walls.

When Louis Philippe inherited Amboise, the castle was restored to a new splendour, with thorough renovations and the return of the royal court to its rooms. Today the presence of numerous portraits and beautiful furniture in period style provides a taste of the magnificence of that happy period. Marie Amélie de Bourbon, wife of Louis Philippe also lived here (below left, with two of her sons, painted in 1831 by Louis Hersent). Naturally the children of the royal couple also lived here, including François, prince of Joinville, portrayed below, and his wife, Francesca Carolina of Braganza, a Brazilian princess, both seen here in mid 19th-century works by François Xavier Winterhalter.

A historic episode is commemorated in an elegant and original way at the château of Amboise, in memory of 25 members of the retinue of Emir Abd el-Kader. They had accompanied him here on the occasion of his detention at the estate between 1848 and 1852, and having died here during that brief period, they were buried in the park of the castle. In 2005, landscape planner Rachid Karaïchi created a memorial as well as a garden of meditation and contemplation, called the "Oriental Garden" in which 25 stones are engraved with quotations that speak of peace and tolerance, taken from the Koran. Each stone also bears the full name carved in stylized letters, of one of the deceased. The variety of plants and the symbolism is also intended to highlight the cultural influences of the Mediterranean and the universal values of tolerance to which Abd el-Kader himself adhered.

The chapel of St Hubert and the lovely stained glass windows by Max Ingrand with scenes from the life of St Louis.

From 1848 to 1852 the château of Amboise had an unexpected guest, the Arabian emir Abd-el-Kader, who spent four years here until Napoleon III, prince and president, personally came to Amboise on October 16, 1852 to communicate his newly acquired liberty.

In 1974, when it was created, the St-Louis Foundation took over the administration of the château and now continues to carry out the restoration which was begun at the end of the last war.

TOURS

Founded by the Romans in the first half of the I century A.D., the town was renamed *Caesarodunum* and was one of the many settlements established by the emperor Augustus to protect the Roman territories which here bordered with those of the Gallic population of the Turones. The area chosen was subject to flooding, but this did not stop the town developing to such an extent that when, in the III century, it was devastated by a barbaric raid which led to a rapid decline, it boasted three thousand inhabitants, a large temple, an amphitheatre and the new name of *Civitas Turonum*.

After a long period of decline, Tours was reborn as an important religious centre created by successive bishops, first and foremost St-Martin, who died here in 397. It flourished particularly under Charlemagne, was sacked by the Normans, and became a hereditary earldom of the d'Anjou family; it was only reconquered for France by Philippe Auguste in 1204. At the time, the town was actually divided into two clearly distinct sectors: Tours itself and the more flourishing suburb of Châteauneuf. In 1356, the inhabitants reunited the two settlements within a single circuit of walls, thus giving origin to the Tours which in 1461, under Louis XI, became the capital of the kingdom. It was this king who promoted the silk industry in Touraine, destined to become the most important factor in the development of the entire region. Thus, until 1540, Tours underwent a period of great economic, artistic, architectural and demographic prosperity. But when, in the 16th century, the Kings of France began to prefer first Blois then Paris as their residence, the town plunged into a rapid and irreversible decline, accentuated by the crisis in the silk industry, caused by the revocation of the Edict of Nantes in 1685.

Few events have marked the history of Tours since then: oc-

An industrious capital of the Kingdom of France for over a century, proudly displaying and carefully protecting its veritable gallery of antique and historic buildings which represent an architectural heritage of different styles and periods, in 1988 Tours earned the title of "City of Art and History". Together with the entire Loire Valley, in 2000 it was added to the official UNESCO list of places considered to be World Heritage sites in the context of cultural landscapes.

Above the distinctive façades of characteristic houses in Touraine, with contrasting wooden latticing. Below, the elegant town hall.

cupied by the Prussians in 1871, it was seriously damaged by bombing raids in 1940 and 1944. After the war, the Dorian brothers, architects, proposed a reconstruction plan aimed at respecting and exploiting the existing historical buildings. Thus, while the modern city continues to develop, it is still possible to admire the remains of the **Gallic-Roman town-walls**, the characteristic district of the **cathedral of St Gatien** (13-16th c.), with the **abbey church of St Julien**, the **tower of Guise**, the **Châteauneuf district**, with the basilica and tomb of St Martin, the **fountain of Beaune**, the **church of Notre-Dame-la-Riche** (15-16th c.), the **Hôtel Gouin**, and the interesting **Museum of Fine Arts** in the ancient archbishopric.

Although looking towards the future, as is evident in the recent and innovative urban structures, Tours is however still proud of its past history represented by places and traditions such as the ancient houses in the Place Plumereau district and the Charlemagne Tower, or the sturdy castle and the magnificent Place Jean Jaurès. In 1996 the splendour of this impressive series of monuments was further enhanced by a futuristic system of lighting, the ambitious "Plan Lumière" designed to create an extraordinary and magical atmosphere in the heart of the city, completely transcending time and space.

The remains of the priorate of St-Cosme. Right, a view of the château of Plessis-lès-Tours.

St-Cosme

The ancient hermitage, transformed in the 11th century into a priory, was restored in the 15th century by Louis XI and had some illustrious guests: Agnès Sorel, Catherine de' Medici, Henry III and the poet Ronsard, who was commendatory prior and is buried here. After the suppression of the priorate, in 1742, the church was demolished, and the other buildings rapidly fell into a state of ruin.

Plessis-lès-Tours

The castle of Plessis-les-Tours is located in the town of La Riche on the outskirts of Tours. In the 11th century it was a fortress which stood between the Loire, the Cher and the Rio Ste-Anne which connected the two rivers. Louis XI purchased it in 1467 and three years later he brought 17 Italian workmen to the castle to set up the first silk factory in Tours. Throughout its history the castle has been put to various uses: it became a hospice for the poor, a factory for hunting pellets, a farm and warehouse until the 20th century, when it was restored and transformed into a pharmaceutical vaccine factory. Considerably restored during the past two centuries, externally the remaining portion of the building corresponds to the southern portion of the former

royal residence built of brick and stone. There is a **museum** dedicated **to St Francis of Paola**, who founded the order of the Minim Friars and built the first French abbey of his order on the royal estate at Plessis.

Below left, the cylindrical 12th-century tower, flanked by the Holy Chapel, stands out in the Renaissance profile of the château of Châteaudun. Bottom, a detail of the famous Renaissance staircase.

the neo-Gothic appearance of its east façade to the architect Parent, who was commissioned to create it in 1886 by Duke Lévis-Mirepoix. The entire château is the result of a rebuilding carried out between 1475 and 1495 by Jacques de Renty, after the previous fortress, built in the 12th century, was almost completely demolished in 1415. The delightful towers also date to the 15th century. Restored in 1831 by the Prince of Montmorency-Laval, the façade overlooks a particularly charming and beautifully tended park.

VENDÔME

The castle of Vendôme stands at the southern boundary of this lovely city of art, in a setting which has remained relatively unspoilt. In 1030 Geoffroi

The château of Montigny.

CHÂTEAUDUN

Located on a calcareous promontory overlooking the valley, the château of Châteaudun was built in the 10th century by the Counts of Blois, to whom it belonged until 1391, when it was bought by Duke Louis d'Orléans along with the entire earldom of Blois and Dunois. In 1439, the château passed to the duke's natural son, John, the *beau Dunois*, famous for heroically fighting against the English alongside Joan of Arc. The property remained in the possession of his descendants until the 18th century when it was inherited by the Dukes of Luynes. In 1938 it was purchased by the State, which carried out thorough restoration work. Only a majestic circular tower remains of the ancient fortress of the Counts of Blois, alongside which stands the Holy Chapel, built in the 15th century.

MONTIGNY

Surroounded by plants and trees, richly furnished and still inhabited, the château of Montigny owes

rise above the gardens. The Beauce gate is quite impressive, while the large romantic garden is the ideal setting for a stroll among the ruins.

Near the banks of the Loire, the massive ruins of the château of Vendôme, strewn amongst the luxuriant gardens, still stand out. Of particular interest is the Beauce gate.

Martel built the first castle-fortress. In 1037 Anne de Bourgogne ordered the construction of the Collegiate Church of St George inside the castle walls. In the 12th century the wooden palisades were replaced by a stone wall and at the same time, the eastern door was built along with the Poitiers tower. In the 15th century the upper part was entirely altered and the internal arrangement modified. In the 17th century César de Vendôme built the access ramp, opened the Beauce gate on the south and erected a long building to the east. The castle became a palace where balls and fêtes were held. After the death of César de Vendôme in 1665 it remained vacant and the Revolution brought it to a state of ruin. The castle was the residence of the Counts and Dukes de Vendôme. In 1170 it hosted Henry II of England, in 1227 Blanche de Castille, and the future King and Saint Louis and

Francis II and Mary Stuart in 1560. Antoine de Bourbon and Jeanne d'Albret, the parents of Henry IV, were buried in the Collegiate Church of St-George. Some of the ruined portions are of considerable interest. The remains of the first donjon date from the 11th century. The Poitiers Tower (12th and 15th centuries) still has nearly all its internal structures. The four semicircular towers built on 12th-century revetments

LAVARDIN

The first castle on this site was built in 1030 and it became the main stronghold of the Counts de Vendôme during the 12th century. Because of its location on the border between the holdings of the Capetian Kings of France and the Kings of Anjou, it was to play an important role in many events. In 1188, after having taken Troo and Montoire, Henry II of England and his son, Richard the Lion-Heart, mounted an unsuccessful siege of the castle. In the 15th and 16th centuries the buildings were remodelled. In 1589 it was taken over by the troops of the Catholic League; in 1590 it was besieged and conquered by the Prince of Conti, commander of the forces of King Henry IV. The king, who as Duke de Vendôme owned the castle, ordered it destroyed.

Though severely damaged by the elements, the ruins situated on a plateau above the Loire Valley still give a clear idea of the three circles of walls around the small castle (16th century) and the 26-metre tall rectangular tower (11th century) which was flanked by two equally tall towers in the 12th century.

Well worth a visit is the church of St Genest at the foot of the castle, where there are interesting murals from the 12th to 16th centuries.

Above left, the rectangular tower (11th c.), one of the best preserved remains of the château which still proudly stand at the top of a hill (left). Top, an interior of the archaic church of St-Genest.

CINQ-MARS-LA-PILE

The castle is situated on a rocky spur in the village of Cinq-Mars-la-Pile (between Tours and Langeais), on the banks of the Loire. In 1230 the St-Médard family began construction of a new castle over the ruins of an older one. In the 14th and 15th centuries the De Rouge and De Châteaugiron families built the buttresses. In the 16th century Louis II de la Trémoïlle, a soldier who participated in the Italian war, modernized the castle, though it was dismantled in the following century. Between 1840 and 1860 Bussiènne, a horticulturist, designed and planted the gardens, also demolishing the main portion of the building. During the Revolution the castle belonged to the famous Luynes family. Originally, the castle was encircled by walls and four 13th-century towers, only two of which remain today. The only other remaining part of the castle is the "salle d'armes" of the King's Master of the Horse (17th century). The turret of the large tower, the large square room on the third floor, the double windows and fireplaces are all part of the work carried out in the 14th and 15th centuries. Dry moats surround the chateau and a bridge connects the towers to the courtyard. The castle gardens are quite fascinating with their thick woods, intriguing maze, carefully trimmed box hedges and well laid-out paths.

Right, one of the two 13th-century towers, the last remains of the sturdy fortification which used to surround the elegant residence of Cinq-Mars-la-Pile.

LANGEAIS

Thanks to its position on the western side of Tours, on the banks of a river, Langeais was of considerable strategic importance both as a fortress blocking access to the capital of the province as well as an outpost against aggressors from the west. Evidence of this is to be found in the ruins of Fulk Nerra's bastion which date to the 10th century and are in what is now the park of the castle. Only the walls on the east and north are still extant. The other two walls of the bastion, which was in the form of an elongated rectangle, were demolished in 1841. Its a consequence of the marriage between Henry Plantagenet and Eleanor of Aquitaine, Langeais became one of the outposts of the vast French possessions of the English king which included the regions of the Loire, Normandy and Aquitaine. The Capetian monarchy, in the war which followed, was to be saved by the internal struggles of the Plantagenets which Philippe Auguste skilfully manipulated. Taking advantage of the assassination of the Duke of Bretagne, perpetrated by John Lackland, son of Henry Plantagenet, Philippe Auguste brought the assassin to trial before the court of Paris and, encouraged by his victories, deprived him of his French possessions. From this moment on Langeais was part of the French royal holdings even though it was ceded various times as guarantee. In the course of the 13th century, custody of Langeais was entrusted successively to Guillaume des Roches, Hugues Lusignan, Alphonse of France, brother of St-Louis, Pierre de la Brosse, Chamberlain of Philip the Bold who, accused of complicity with the King of

Castile then at war with France, was hanged at Montfaucon in 1278.

During the Hundred Years' War, Langeais fell into the hands of the English more than once. In 1428 they abandoned it upon receiving ransom, on condition that "the castle be torn down and razed to the ground, except the large tower". Aware of the need to build a new fortress on this same site, Louis XI entrusted the direction of the works to his personal counsellor Jean Bourré, who also held the office of "Captain of Langeais". With its high walls and its narrow cross-bar windows its three round towers and its encircling wall of machicolations and crenellations, the new building is the perfect picture of an imposing austere fortress. One of the characteristics of this façade is the continuity of the sentinel walk which surrounds the entire building, towers included, for a length of 130 metres, always on the same level. The king's purpose in rebuilding this castle was that of protecting the royal residences to the west - Tours, Plessis-lès-Tours and Amboise - which were vital to his government. To the east they were protected by Chaumont and to the south by Chinon and Loches. On the 6th of December, 1491, the castle of Langeais was the stage for an event that was to make it more famous than any other castle – the wedding of Charles VIII and Anne de Bretagne, as a result of which Brittany was annexed to France. This union was to throw European politics into confusion. The duchess Anne had already been married by proxy to Maximilian of Austria, Emperor of the Holy Roman Empire, and Charles VIII was engaged to his daughter Margaret of Austria, who with this wedding in mind, had been brought up at the court of

The west façade of the château.

Taken as a whole the castle mirrors the soul of its builder, the fearsome Fulk Nerra, Count of Anjou, nicknamed in his time "The Black Hawk". He was a typical example of the feudal outlaw: ferocious, perfidious and cynical with an insatiable lust for power. At the same time he was endowed with a superstitious piety and was famous for his excesses. His gifts as strategist and statesman permitted this founder of the Angevin dynasty to continue in power for fifty years.

When, under the reign of Hugh Capet, Fulk took possession of the holdings of Eudes I, Count of Blois and of Tours, he had this fortress built as a point of support at the top of a promontory-shaped hill enclosed by the valleys of the Loire and of the Roumer at their confluence. After his death, the house of Anjou continued its unrelenting course which was to culminate in 1154 in the consecration as King of England of Henry of Anjou, called Plantagenet.

France. The union had been planned by the regent Anne de Beaujeu who wanted to unite Brittany to the French kingdom and was conscious of the danger of letting it fall into the hands of the Emperor (even if, as Duke of Bretagne, he was a vassal of the king). The situation had precipi-

tated. Charles VIII did not present himself to the duchess at Rennes, which was besieged by French troops, until a few days before the ceremony. In order to escape the opposing party, the princess arrived secretly at the castle of Langeais, where the king was waiting for her. This wedding was more like a kidnapping than anything else. The most important clauses in the wedding contract were the unification of Brittany with France, and, to ensure this union, the obligation on the part of the queen, if the king died before she did and left no heirs, to marry his successor. And this was just what hap-

pened. A second marriage made her the wife of Louis XII. The chroniclers of the time have left us fantastic accounts of the pomp and magnificence of the wedding. After this, Langeais disappears from the mainstream of history. The château came through the Revolution intact, and in 1797 it was acquired by a burger of Tours, Charles-François Moisant, who left it in a state of abandon. Houses were built right against the walls of the castle and the finest hall on the ground floor was transformed into a stable for the gendarmes. Bought in 1839 by a Parisian lawyer, Christophe Baron, the building underwent

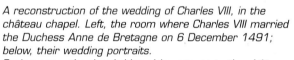

*A reconstruction of the wedding of Charles VIII, in the
château chapel. Left, the room where Charles VIII married
the Duchess Anne de Bretagne on 6 December 1491;
below, their wedding portraits.
Facing page, the drawbridge giving access to the château.*

radical restoration. Jacques Siegfried, who bought the castle
in 1886, set about restructuring it fundamentally. The most
important aspect was the restoration of the interior, to which
he dedicated twenty years of his life.

The unity of style which the castle owed to the speed with
which it had been built survived the centuries. While this
may have been true of the exterior it was not the case with the
inside and Jacques Siegfried, who was an enthusiast of history,
took the castle to heart, set out to restore the interior of the
monument to what it must have looked like when it was built.
With this end in mind he engaged a talented young architect,
Lucien Roy, and the most famous archaeologists such as
Palustre, Foulc, Spitzer, Peyre and Bonafé. Their attempts
to be as historically exact as possible led them to search
particularly for elements of flamboyant Gothic style. The furniture and wood panelling is either authentic or copied from
originals. The pavements, which differ from room to room,
were designed from examples of the 15th century or copied
from period paintings. They are the most noteworthy aspect
of the restoration, for the furniture, with few exceptions, is all
period. Wardrobes, chests, bureaus are either 15th century or
Renaissance.

Above, a bedroom on the first floor of the château with an oak bed and Latin inscription on the canopy: "Post tenebras spero lucem" (I hope to find the light after the darkness), late 15th century. Left, the royal bedroom with the canopied bed. Below, the 15th-century wedding chest of the duchess Anne de Bretagne.

But the highlight of the interior decoration is the marvellous *collection of 14th and 15th-century tapestries* – over thirty – which Jacques Siegfried assembled between 1888 and 1900.

The oldest pieces, including various millefleur and a splendid *Crucifixion*, are Flemish, while the others are mostly Aubusson. The intrinsic value of these works of art, including sculpture and paintings, is intensified by the fact that they harmonize perfectly with the furniture. This inviting and homely aspect of the château strikes the visitor in sharp contrast to the forbidding aspect of the fortress from outside.

In 1904 Jacques Siegfried offered to donate the château and his collections to the French Institute. For fear that this example of the national patrimony might be bought by some wealthy art lover from the New World and

transported stone by stone to America, the Institute decided to accept the financial burden that maintaining a monument of similar size entailed.

In fact, the continuous growth of tourism and the position of Langeais on the route of the châteaux of the Loire were to provide the Siegfried Foundation with the means not only of maintaing the monument, but also providing for the periodic restoration required. The French Institute ensures that its management is completely autonomous, with the aid – for some of the works of restoration – of the Caisse Nationale des Monuments Historiques et des Sites.

In 1924, and again in 1938, Jacques Siegfried's daughter, Agnès, continued her father's work, donating the large park which, beyond the ruins of Fulk Nerra's tower, dominates the valley of the Loire to the west – with the houses which climb up the slopes of the hill – and on the northwest the road that leads to the upland plain.

The monument is thus amply protected on this side. To the east and to the north, the old city embraces the château and provides a suitable environment. In line with the spirit of the donor and its own principles, the French Institute promises to persevere and continue his work.

Above right and below, three Tournai tapestries (early 16th-cent.) depicting a deer hunt; above left, the famous Flemish tapestry known as "aux aristoloches."

VILLANDRY

This elegant Renaissance château stands not far from the Loire and from ancient prehistoric menhirs. Originally a feudal stronghold stood on the spot where Philippe Auguste King of France and Henry II Plantagenet King of England met on July 4, 1189. Their contrasts were arbitrated in the medieval tower that still stands in the southwest corner of the castle. Philippe Auguste won and his victory was then sanctioned by the peace of Azay. A few centuries later the manor became the property of Jean le Breton, president of the Chamber of the Counts of Blois. Minister for Francis I, Jean was charged by the king with overseeing the construction of the royal palaces of Fontainebleau and Chambord, since he was well-versed in architecture. For himself, Jean le Breton (whose family originally came from Scotland) set out to build a palace which was just the opposite of the foreboding feudal castle.

The older structures, with the exception of the keep, were razed to the ground and in 1536 the construction of a new building with a U-shaped ground plan around a court of honour facing the valley of the Loire was begun. The two large L-shaped wings contain typically Renaissance elements borrowed from the palaces built at the beginning of the 16th century: large windows framed by pilasters with capitals in classic style, horizontal mouldings, large dormer windows decorated with superstructures enhanced by pediments and volutes.

The wide façades were enlivened with slight asymmetries (in the placing of the windows, the length and angle of the wings) and by the arched porticoes on two sides of the courtyard.

The ornamental gardens are unusual in that the multicolored, geometric patterns are created using only vegetables and fruit plants.

Joachim Carvallo

When, in 1906, Doctor Joachim Carvallo, born in Spain in 1869, bought Villandry which would have been demolished otherwise, the château was surrounded by an English park, which had replaced the traditional gardens during the 19th century. At the time Carvallo was about to embark on a promising scientific career under the aegis of one of the foremost intellectuals, professor Charles Richet who was to become a Nobel prize-winner in 1913. But Villandry took his life over with the force of a genuine passion and clearly disrupted the best-laid plans. Slowly but surely, Carvallo increasingly distanced himself from the world of science, choosing to dedicate his life completely to Villandry. Thus his passionate interest brought into being the splendid gardens, conceived to be in complete harmony with the Renaissance architecture of the château. The ornamental vegetable gardens too were created and early on, during the First World War, were used to provide sufficient food for hospital patients. This garden was to become Carvallo's favourite place, where more than 250,000 vegetables and flowering plants formed a stupendous decorative open-air fresco. It was the job of nine gardeners to replace the plants to preserve intact the harmonious arrangement of colours as the seasons inexorably changed. Today over 40 different species combine to perpetuate this extraordinary natural work of art, which Carvallo, ahead of the times in this initiative too, desired to open to the public, offering it to the admiration of all.

Above, one of the three buildings framing the courtyard forming a large "U."

Below, another view of the splendid and spectacular garden.

Partially surrounded by a moat fed by ground water, the castle was landscaped with large gardens laid out on three different levels.

Landscape gardening developed together with the Italian Renaissance and was conceived of as a pendant to the architecture. At the time, Italian style gardens were characterized by a geometric layout and a typically architectonic taste. In France, this new fashion led to the creation of the "French garden", where the garden became larger, eliminating the perimetral walls and limiting the architectural structures in general. Convenient avenues ran along the flower beds where low hedge borders set off the decorative plants. The gardens of Villandry are perfect examples of this concept – they are all large and are set on various terraces. Water is collected on the topmost level while a middle terrace lies on the same plane as the rooms on the ground floor of the castle (ornamental garden) and a lower level contains the ornamental vegetable gardens. The upper terrace, which extends to a wood of tall trees, consists of orchards crisscrossed by shady paths.

In line with this principle, the entire park of Villandry is cut through by green galleries, placed higher than the neighboring gardens so that they can be seen from above. The ornamental garden on the middle terrace in the part nearest the castle consists of the so-called "gardens of love". Here four large squares of box shrubs and flowers form motifs which symbolize the allegories of love. The square to the northwest, with its wounded hearts arranged according to the allegory of the ball, indicates passionate love, while the northeast square with fans, horns and billets-doux (at the centre) represents adulterous love, dominated by yellow flowers. Tender love is symbolized in the southwest, with hearts separated by flames of love and by the masks worn for balls, while the last square on the southeast evokes tragic love with sword blades and the blood-red colour of duels.

The southernmost part of the garden contains three large diamond-shaped beds enclosing the crosses of Languedoc, Malta and Béarn. Beyond the moat, lower down, the ornamental vegetable gardens lie between the castle and the edge of the town, with the Romanesque church in the

The kitchen with terracotta tiles was restored in 2000.

corner. This part of the park is unique in the way in which the geometric designs of the large multicoloured beds are created exclusively by vegetables and fruit plants. Long ago, in the 16th century, when the first botanic gardens were created, previously unknown plants were introduced from the Americas. Considered rarities, they were planted in the most prestigious gardens in Europe and were carefully tended so that they might adapt to the new climate. This was also what happened in Villandry and the original aspect of the nine large sections of the vegetable garden have been perfectly reconstructed thanks to the initiative of Dr. Joachim Carvallo, who replanted the old gardens in the early 1900s basing his work on drawings by the landscape painter Androuet du Cerceau. Each vegetable garden creates geometrical motifs in which colours are provided by the leaves of cabbages, carrots, beets and lettuce. Apple and pear trees whose branches form lattices define and separate the beds. The gravel paths – like the centre of the nine squares – are decorated with small fountains which were originally used for irrigation.

From top to bottom: a bedroom furnished with 18th-century pieces, the dining room with its marble floors and the "chambre du Potager" bedroom.

Right, the bedroom of Prince Jérôme Bonaparte (1784-1860) who bought the château but never lived there.

AZAY-LE-RIDEAU

The château of Azay-le-Rideau is situated on an enchanting bend of the Indre river. Most probably the name Azay derives from the Latin *Asiacus*, the name of the owner of these lands, and the village of Azay dates back to Roman times. In the Middle Ages, thanks to the presence of a small fortress, it stood watch over the local ford across the Indre. In the 12th century the owner was Rideau or Ridel d'Azay, whose fierceness earned him the nickname "Child of the Devil". Henry II Plantagenet expropriated all his lands, but they were later restored, together with the castle, by Philippe Auguste to Rideau's son, Hugues, knight of Turenne, who served the king faithfully in the battle of Bouvines. Later, in the early 15th century, the castle seems to have been in the hands of the Duke of Burgundy. When the duke offended the Dauphin Charles (future Charles VII) and his army, a military attack was launched against the stronghold in 1418: the garrison composed of 354 persons was wiped out and the castle and nearby town were burned down and completely destroyed. The present château was built a century later on the area of the earlier building. A historical panorama of the late 15th century helps to explain the characteristics of the new building. At that time Charles VIII and Louis XII organized military expeditions to Italy where they were impressed by the art and architecture they found there. As a result many artists and craftsmen were called to France in the employ of the king and his followers.

Their mark is most clearly to be seen in the region of the Loire where the royal court resided from the time of Charles VII on. The Italianate style of the châteaux of Amboise and of the remodelling of the castle of Blois was soon copied in the residences of the old noble families and in those of the aspiring nobility. Gilles Berthelot, the owner of a part of the territory of Azay-le-Rideau at the beginning of the 16th century, was just such a man, an important financier whose father, Martin Berthelot, had been Maître de la Chambre des Finances for Louis XI and Charles VIII. Gilles, in a brilliant career, became a counsellor to the king, Maître de la Chambre des Comptes and mayor of Tours. Thanks to his marriage with Philippa Lesbahy, who owned the rest of the territory of Azay, he was able to reunite the entire estate under one owner and begin construction of the grandiose castle. With the financial and political backing of various relatives who held important posts, Gilles Berthelot began the reconstruction of the medieval manor in 1518. That summer, under the supervision of master builder Etienne Rousseau, as many as 120 labourers were at work preparing the foundations. What was left of the previous stronghold had to be eliminated and the area then had to be drained before setting up the wooden pilings on which the whole building rests. Cream-coloured tufa from the Cher valley was used for the building itself. The blocks were carried on barges as far as Port-aux-Chalands near Vallères and then transported on wagons for the remaining ten kilometres. The château has an unusual L-shaped ground plan and its architectural details reveal the evolution from the Gothic to the Renaissance style

The château reflected in the waters of the Indre, surrounded by lush plane trees, and, facing page, above right, the façade: behind it is the grand staircase.

and a new concept of the dwelling which is no longer a stronghold but a pleasant residence. Only an occasional element of military architecture, lightened by a Renaissance imprint, remains side by side with a few elements that are still Gothic, like the high-pitched slate roofs. This was due as much to the taste of Philippa, who kept close track of the proceedings and supervised the construction work, conferring an exquisitely feminine touch to the building, as it was to the work of the master builder Rousseau, the sculptor Pierre Maupoint and the carpenter Jacques Thoreau. Seen from the outside, the castle has corner towers set on walls which jut out from the main building and which are linked together on the outside by a sentinel walk. This was built out of respect for the preceding tradition and has no function at all in a castle without an enclosed courtyard. Numerous references to the Italian Renaissance are to be found side by side with elements which imitate the dwellings of the older French nobility. The pilasters with their capitals which support the horizontal cornices, the superstructures of the dormer windows with pediments, volutes and shell-shaped clouds, and the overall symmetry reveal an Italianate classicizing inspiration. This is also the case of the staircase of honour, entrance to which is through twin doors surmounted by reliefs of Francis I's salamander and the ermine of Claude of France. The three upper levels of the staircase are characterized by straight flights with landings which lead to the mullioned Italianate loggias which overlook the garden below. The ceilings over the stairs have stone coffering bordered by arches in which the portraits of the 15th and 16th-century kings and queens were sculpted in the 19th century. The innovation of this staircase makes it one of the key points of French Renaissance architecture – under the stimulus of new concepts, the narrow spiral staircase of medieval origin was abandoned. Broad straight flights of stairs became popular, no longer illuminated by narrow louvers but by large loggias which provide a view over the park as well as letting in light. There are various rooms inside the château on the ground floor (the royal room and the red room) as well as more all-purpose rooms and a kitchen. The first floor contains a dining room, a ball room, and a blue room as well as those of Francis I and of Claude of France. Gilles Berthelot never finished the construction work on the castle. His cousin Semblançay, who was Superintendent of Finances, was accused of having stolen public funds, found guilty, and hanged in Montfaucon. Gilles found himself in a difficult situation and thought it wise to flee while there

Above, the grand ballroom with its elegant Flemish tapestries.

Right, the grand staircase leading to the interior, inspired by the Italian style, is decorated with coats of arms and emblems of the château's various owners.

Below, the bedroom of the lord where Gothic and Renaissance styles blend harmoniously.

Left, a 16th-century wedding chest.

Facing page, the salamander, symbol of Francis I dominates the monumental fireplace in the room named for the King.

was still time. In 1527 he sought refuge in the free city of Metz where he died in exile ten years later. The castle, with all its lands, was confiscated by Francis I and given to the captain of the guards, Antoine Raffin, who carried the work to completion. Later, when the royal seat was definitively removed to Paris by Francis I, Touraine's importance diminished. The château of Azay-le-Rideau belonged to the families of Cossé de Gonnord, St-Gelais de Lusignan, Vassé. In 1871, after the defeat of the French army, Prussian troops were quartered in the castle which had been requisitioned from the fourth Marquis of Biencourt, owner at the time of the château. In that year, on the 19th of February, Prince Frederick Charles of Prussia was housed there with his general staff. The tale goes that during supper, which was eaten in the kitchen, a heavy chandelier fell from the keystone in the ceiling onto the prince's table and almost killed him. Frederick thought it was an attempt on his life and the officers had a hard time persuading him not to set fire to the castle in retaliation. The building later became once more the property of the Marquises of Biencourt who sold it in 1904 when the society they administered went bankrupt. The new owner, M. Arteau, sold the château to the State for the sum of 200,000 francs. The building has since been restored while the park and the bend of the Indre again look as they originally did. The rooms inside have been turned into a **Renaissance Museum** thanks to the recovery of furniture, tapestries, objects of daily use and paintings. Among the material exhibited, mention should be made of the canopied bed which belonged to the king's marshal, Pierre de Filley de la Barre, who died in the siege of Nice in 1705. This piece of furniture, marked by an animated floral decoration in silk, is in the blue room, while another tester bed with damask, originally in the castle of Effiat, is in the red room. Other pieces of Renaissance furniture in wood fur-

nish the rooms of the castle: the chest in Francis I's room is decorated with small pilasters and with fantastic animals on either side of the two medallions, while in the kitchen is an elegant chest with two profiles carved on the front. The kitchen also contains examples of cupboards and utensils in ceramics and in metal, such as grills, fire tongs, forks, basins and pitchers. The collection of tapestries in Azay-le-Rideau includes the 16th-century tapestry of the *Three Fates* executed in Brussels, which is on exhibit in the ballroom near another tapestry of the same period with plant motifs.

On the other walls of this room are four large 17th-century tapestries of Flemish production with biblical scenes such as the *Reconciliation of Esau and Jacob*, the *Judgement of Solomon*, the *Ark of the Covenant*, and the *Visit of the Queen of Sheba to Solomon*. In the dining room on the ground floor are 16th-century Flemish tapestries with the *Queen Semiramis*, the king's messenger and *Balthazar's feast*. The tapestries in the royal chamber, designed by Simon Vouet, represent the *Love story of Rinaldo and Armida*. The two tapestries with the palaces of Vincennes and Versailles, in the blue room, come from the Lille workshop, while those with hunting scenes come from Beauvais. To make the museum more complete, these rooms also contain numerous paintings with the portraits of the Kings of France and members of the royal family, including Francis I, Henry II, Catherine de' Medici, Francis II, Charles IX, Henry III, Margaret of Valois and Louis XIV.

Inside, the rooms were redone in the 19th century to make them more comfortable. In the salon, the dining-room and Balzac's bedroom there is wallpaper from 1803 that has been carefully restored or remade. The entire suite has been made into a very interesting **Balzac Museum.**

SACHÉ

The castle of Saché was built between the end of the 15th and the beginning of the 16th century, over the foundations of a small, 12th-century manor. In the 15th century it was owned by the Rousseley family. In the 18th century it was transformed, and specifically a large staircase was built. In the 19th century the owner, De Margonne, transformed the castle: he had the window mullions removed and suspended ceilings installed in all the rooms.

Honoré de Balzac lived at De Margonne's castle and it was there that he wrote many of his famous novels: *Louis Lambert*, *Le Père Goriot* (Father Goriot), *La Recherche de l'Absolu* (The Quest of the Absolute); *Les Illusions Perdues* (Lost Illusions); *César Birroteau*, and *Le Lys dans la Vallée* (The Lilly of the Valley).

Externally, this 16th-century manor house still has one of its original 12th-century towers. A new tower was built in the 18th century with a straight inside staircase that replaced the 16th-century spiral steps.

Left, one of the oldest parts of the château of Saché. Below, the elegant architecture of the château of Ussé.

An aerial view of the château of Ussé.

USSÉ

The castle of Ussé, on the edge of the forest of Chinon, stands on an area that was already occupied in ancient times, as shown by the remains of tumulus tombs found nearby. The fort that was built here in the Middle Ages was square in plan with towers and belonged to the descendants of Guilduin de Saumur. In the 15th century, when the royal seat was in Chinon, the castle belonged to Jeanne, daughter of the king Charles VIII and of Agnès Sorel, his mistress. When Jeanne married Antoine de Bueil, other towers and architectonic elements were added to the dwelling. Jean III de Bueil, Jean IV who fell at Azincourt, and Jean V known as "the scourge of the English", courageous warrior in Normandy and Admiral of France, all lived at Ussé. They built the 15th-century part of the castle, including the external

façades, in various stages. When Charles VII died, the Bueil family fell into disgrace: Jean V openly rebelled and sided with the League. In 1485 he ceded the castle to the house of Espinay, a noble Breton family which restructured the complex, as did the Valentinay family later.

The new Renaissance influences caused the new owners to demolish the wing which shut out the panorama towards the valley and to change the aspect of the façades. The interiors were also rebuilt and lower ceilings were installed. The Renaissance chapel in the park was built between 1520 and 1538 by Charles d'Espinay and his wife Lucrezia de Pons. Other works later involved the part of the castle which opened onto the court of honour and the side towards the valley where an Italianate pavilion overlooking the terraced gardens was made.

A royal chamber was prepared inside the palace in case the king should come for a

Still flourishing and lived in, the chateau contains a great number of furnishings of great historical value: the royal chamber looks as it did in the 18th century, while an antechamber contains a valuable 16th-century Italian cabinet with intarsia.

The gallery on the ground floor has a collection of weapons and various Flemish tapestries, while other tapestries from Brussels are exhibited in the drawing room. Numerous paintings and pottery are to be seen at Ussé as well as a majolica *Virgin and Child* by Luca della Robbia.

Below, pastel portrait of the Duchess of Duras by Jean Valade (1710-1787).

Above, a painting attributed to Pierre Mignan, portrait of Mademoiselle de Blois, daughter of Louis XIV and Louise de la Vallière (17th century). Left, detail of a silk dress with tassels (18th century).

visit, although as chance would have it he never did. After the Revolution, which left the castle untouched, Ussé passed into the hands of the Duchess of Duras, Claire de Kersaint, who formed a literary circle here, then into the hands of the Countess of Rochejacquelin and finally into those of the de Blacas family, to whose descendants it still belongs. The particularly elegant, fairy-tale appearance of this castle at the edge of a dark, mysterious forest seems to have influenced Charles Perrault's conception of the castle in his "Sleeping Beauty".

Above left, the king's bedroom with the Polish style bed (18th century) and with furniture dating from around 1770; and, above right, a view of the staircase with the Italian style wrought iron railing by the architect François Mansard, with an 18th-century sedan.

Right, Louis XV Chinese lacquer corner cabinet.

Left, Florentine cabinet inlaid with mother-of-pearl and ivory (16th century). In the background, Bruxelles tapestries with scenes from David and Goliath.

CHINON

The château overlooking the Vienne, and, left, the clock tower.

This château was originally built in stone in 954 by Theobald I, Count of Blois, on a steep plateau. The stronghold, which replaced a lighter wooden structure, then passed to the rival Count of Anjou, Geoffroi Martel, in 1044. The Count of Anjou was the first to join the walls of the two original defensive structures (the castles of Milieu and of Coudray) as well as adding towers and the chapel of St-Melanie. The far east wing was added by Henry II Plantagenet, who descended from the Counts of Anjou and the King of England; he called it "St. Georges's fort" dedicating it to the English patron saint. With the beginning of the long war with France, the English stronghold passed under the crown of Philippe Auguste in June of 1205. Reconstruction was immediately begun on the towers of the Guards and of the Dogs, the new walls and the large moat which separates the western and the central blocks. Additions continued to be made up to the 15th century when the royal apartments and great throne room were realized. The dauphin Charles made Chinon his residence and received Joan of Arc here in 1429. The story is told of how Charles mingled with the nobles and had another person take his place. Yet Joan recognized him in the crowd and unhesitatingly went up to him saying "Kind Dauphin, the King of Heaven asks that you be crowned at Reims and that you take Orléans…" On assurance that the young woman was neither mad nor possessed by the devil, Charles followed her advice and became Charles VII, defeating his adversaries. Chinon thus became the seat of the royal government. Queen Mary of Anjou and Charles' mistress, Agnès Sorel, lived here. Their apartments were connected to the king's by an underground passage. From Chinon Charles VII reorganized France, abolishing the feudal organization, and under his reign the castle lived its moments of greatest splendour, after which it was abandoned by the court. Even so it was at Chinon that Louis XII received Cesare Borgia, sent by pope Alexander VI to annul the marriage of the King of France with Jeanne, who was lame and hunchbacked. This left Louis XII free to marry Anne de Bretagne, widow of Charles VIII. The château later belonged to Cardinal Richelieu, who left it to his descendants. At this point the ravages of time were augmented by man-made devastation. In 1699 the Duke of Richelieu demolished Charles VII's throne room and other structures considered passé. Neglect then led to the collapse of the roofs and pavements, while various towers fell into ruin. The stones were sold as building material. After having risked total demolishion in 1854, the château has been patiently restored: the floors in the royal apartments have been recreated according to their original design and the rooms have been furnished with copies of antique furniture.

Le Rivau

The castle is located on the edge of the village of Leméré, south of Chinon. The castle's origins date from the 12th-14th century, but no documents have survived to recount its history. In the 15th century ownership passed to the Beauvau family. At the time it was a stark, bare fortress surrounded by moats that framed the cylindrical corner towers. In 1442 Pierre de Beauvau obtained permission from King Charles VII to fortify the castle and made the changes that one can still see today. In the 18th century the moats were filled in and the west wing was demolished to open the main courtyard to the outside (as at Chaumont, Luynes, Ussé). In the 19th century the superb Gothic chapel on the north side was destroyed, and only a few traces remain. In the 20th century the moats were drained and the rooms were restored to their original appearance.

The castle is entered via the tower-gate and the drawbridge. The façade overlooking the courtyard is a blend of charm and harmony, with its Renaissance decorations. Inside, on the ground floor, there are interesting French-style ceilings and stone floors. The floor tiles on the upper storey are Renaissance "cotto". The furniture also dates from the Renaissance and of particular note is the ancient leather wedding chest.

Altogether twelve enchanted gardens surround Rivau but the most outstanding with its magical flourishing plants is the pretty garden of Gargantua, the memorable character of Rabelais' 16th-century work which also immortalized the château of Rivau. The wine-making activity of the castle dates from the same period in the early 16th-century, including the rare old vines (Malvasia, Alicante and Sauvignon blanc) which are still planted and cultivated using traditional methods. "Appetite grows with eating" as Gargantua would say. And "Thirst is quenched by drinking". With such mottoes in mind, as well as painting the walls of the castle with subjects dear to the literary genius Rabelais, the Beauvau family have made their home into a pleasant and convivial centre. Recently restored, the frescoes (especially in the dining hall) still enhance the rooms of the castle where, in addition, some interesting 16th-century presses, also recently restored, are exhibited.

Fontevraud

The Abbey of Fontevraud, one of the most evocative monastery complexes in the whole of France, was founded in 1101 by the hermit Robert d'Abrissel, who wanted to set up a mixed community. The abbey thus separately united in five different buildings (fully autonomous convents) monks and lay brothers, nuns, the sick, lepers and repentant public sinners, all under the authority of an abbess. The order enjoyed rapid and constant fortune, also due to the fact that the abbesses, generally from important families, were able to procure influential protection for the abbey. The Plantagenet kings and queens chose to be buried here, in the abbey church (Henry II, Eleanor of Aquitaine, Richard Lion-Heart and Isabel d'Angoulême). Young men from noble families abandoning the world found refuge in the abbey, and the four daughters of Louis XV were educated here until revolutionaries suppressed the order in 1789. Transformed into a prison by Napoleon, the abbey remained as such until 1963. Today it hosts conferences, seminars, concerts and exhibitions, thanks to an ambitious plan for the recovery and use of its structures. Particularly charming, to this day, in addition to the church in typical Aquitaine style, is the kitchen complex with its numerous chimney-tops and diamond point cut stone roof.

Views of the Abbey of Fontevraud: exterior of the church; the building which housed the kitchens for the entire complex; the polychrome tombs of the Plantagenets.

MONTSOREAU

Today the château of Montsoreau stands a few metres from the banks of the Loire. When it was built in the 15th century, the waters of the river lapped its front. In 1820 the embankments were widened. For Jean de Chambes, the builder and an important personage in the court of Charles VII, it served as a point from which to control the various routes which crossed the area, including that of the pilgrims on their way to the Abbey of Fontevraud. The most famous figure in the history of the castle is without doubt Charles de Chambes immortalized in *La Dame de Monsoreau* by Alexandre Dumas père. Written three centuries after the facts to which it refers took place, the tale was based on the story of Charles, his wife Françoise (and not Diane) and her lover, the lord of Bussy. Françoise de Méridor had taken as her second husband Charles, the Duke of Alençon's chief hunter, who was about the same age as his wife and quite handsome. In the castle of Coutancière, Françoise de Méridor met Louis de Clermont d'Amboise, lord of Bussy and favourite of the Duke of Alençon. He is remembered as being "handsome, with a fine face, clear eyes, a commanding, often seductive, glance", a courageous and cultured warrior and reader of Plutarch. His figure and his often unscrupulous attitudes made him enemies, and in 1579 the lord of Bussy decided to retire to his estate and left the court. This was when he courted the lady of Montsoreau. He boasted of his success – whether or not it corresponded to the truth – in a letter to a friend. The rumour soon reached the ears of De Chambes, who hurried to the castle and

Aerial view of the château and, below, views of the rooms with the permanent exhibit *Les imaginaires de Loire*.

forced his wife, who professed her innocence, to write a note to her presumed lover inviting him to a tryst in the castle of Coutancière. The mortal trap was sprung. Louis de Bussy showed up at the appointment with only one friend and as soon as he entered the castle the doors were blocked to prevent his escape. Attacked by a dozen men, he defended himself to his last breath and, about to throw himself out the window, he was killed. The ending of the tale is rather prosaic, for his death was received with indifference by Françoise de Méridor who, reconciled with her husband, presented him with several children.

Inside the castle, sixteen rooms host the permanent exhibit *Les imaginaires de Loire*, a striking audiovisual itinerary recounting life in the Loire valley. Designed to arouse the curiousity of visitors of all ages, evocative images and plays of light and music recreate the ancient and present-day look of the river and encourage the visitor to explore themes linked to its history and economy—not to mention the many legends associated with the Loire and the castle of Montsoreau.

embellishment, almost like a proud but charming welcome. The unmistakable decorative check pattern alternates stone and brick and is refined by the presence of elegant sculptural elements, including the salamander, one of the symbols of the Loire valley, which dominates the entrance gate. However, the whole château, with its classic sloping roofs, towers, and large windows opening in the sturdy walls, represents a place of great charm, and is a most pleasant destination for an interesting visit.

MONTREUIL-BELLAY

Like many other castles of the Loire, Montreuil was also built on the orders of the Count of Anjou, Fulk Nerra. This XI century warrior was a tireless builder and he had the castle set on a steep slope where it would be easier to defend. The manor was given by Fulk to a vassal, Berlay (or Bellay), who gave his name to the location. Montreuil seems to be derived from the Latin *Monasteriolum* with reference to the small monastery the Du Bellay had built near the stronghold.

At that time the castle consisted of a tall main tower surrounded by moats, and a double circle of walls protected by barbicans.

LES RÉAUX

Just a few kilometers from Bourgueil, in a fertile valley covered by green vineyards, the grapes of which produce excellent red wines, and where the poet Ronsard loved to stay, there is a characteristic and charming château, Les Réaux. Built at the end of the 15th century, the name is linked mainly to its famous eighteenth century owner, Tallemant des Réaux who, with his Historiettes, traced an amusing and accurate portrait of French society at that time.

On approaching the château, the fine detail of its superb decoration is most striking. In particular, the pavilion providing access to the château, in particular, with the two imposing towers flanking it, undoubtedly constitutes its main and rather special

Above, Les Réaux, with its distinctive chequered decoration. Below, aerial view of the château of Montreuil-Bellay.

Montreuil-Bellay: above, the dining room; below, the flamboyant Gothic chapel with interesting 15th-century frescoes.

One of the most illustrious descendants of the Du Bellay family was Guillaume Du Bellay, a warrior and governor of Turin and Piedmont, who used a network of informers spread throughout the courts of Europe in explicating his diplomatic activity. His brother Jean was also active in this field. As a cardinal he lived at length in Rome with his nephew Joachim. The latter, a subtle poet, left us his sense of nostalgia for his country and for the buildings in the Loire valley.

The new lords of Montreuil, the Melun-Tancarville and the d'Harcourt, built the defenses of the city in the 15th century with a circle of walls and gates of which only four are still to be seen.

Thanks to the testament and the money of the d'Harcourt, the castle of Montreuil-Bellay took on its present aspect.

The entrance consists of the Châtelet, followed by the Petit-Château (with four apartments meant for the canons of the chapter) and the Château-Neuf. A square building with low ogee arches, situated in an internal court between the Petit-Château and the Château-Neuf, contains the enormous kitchen. A walkway connects this room to the Château-Neuf, with its fine internal staircase. Besides the chapel, with its fine frescoes, the base of a pyramid, whose purpose is still a mystery, is to be found in the castle – at the base of the western towers of the fort.

SAUMUR

Once upon a time there was a lovely castle, a vacation residence, so beautiful that René of Anjou, the poet king, chose this above all others as the Castle of Love in his romance *Le Coeur d'Amour Epris...*

Thereafter various buildings arose on the emerald rock: one built by Thibault le Tricheur, Count of Blois, and later taken over by the terrible Count of Anjou, Fulk Nerra; and one built by Geoffroi Plantagenet of which remains may still exist at the base of the southeast wing. But the story of

"This splendid castle, a place of joy, was built on an emerald rock, in which there was a vein of sparkling diamonds in such a very great quantity that one could wonder at almost as many or even more diamonds than emeralds. The four slopes of the walls of this beautiful castle were of crystal and crowning each corner was a large tower made of fine and glistening rubies, the smallest of which was bigger than the entire body of a man. And these towers were covered with platinum, as thick as the palm of a hand and the building between the towers was covered with tiles of fine gold beautifully enamelled with the motto of the god of Love, 'A coeur volage...'. And to be even more clearly understood, the beautiful castle had the same aspect as that of Saumur in Anjou which stands along the river Loire." René of Anjou.

The château overlooking the left bank of the Loire.

the present castle begins with the one built by St-Louis. Saumur belonged first to the Counts of Blois, then to the house of Anjou and then to the King of France. In 1203 Philippe Auguste, rival of the Plantagenets, took over the castle and incorporated it and the territory it controlled into the royal possessions. Historians place the construction of a fortress at Saumur between 1227 and 1230, when Blanche of Castile was queen regent. The fortress was to serve the Crown in reconquering Angers and that part of Anjou which it had just lost under the Treaty of Vendôme. Its usefulness from a military point of view lasted only two years, for Angers once more became the royal seat and St-Louis constructed an enormous fortress there which is still standing. We know that "good King René", grandson of Louis I of Anjou, had sung the praises of Saumur as a Castle of Love and had left his mark on it. The accounts and diaries of his director of works, preserved in the National Archives, reveal that the construction work on the castle must have been important to judge from the time involved (from 1454 to 1472) and the cost.

At the death of King René, in 1480, the duchy of Anjou returned to the Crown and the castle of Saumur came to house a royal garrison. A century later the Reformation modified the destiny of the castle: King Henry III was forced to ask the King of Navarre for help in saving his throne and concluded a truce with him. With the Treaty of Tours, he ceded Saumur, where there were many Protestants. The future Henry IV named his ambassador and friend, Philippe Duplessis-Mornay, who was in charge of the negotiations, as military governor general.

NATIONAL RIDING SCHOOL
Le Cadre Noir de Saumur

In addition to the château, Saumur is famous for the National Riding School, the Military Academy and the Cavalry Museum. The riding school, one of the oldest in Europe, originated from the Italian riding school in the 16th century during the Italian wars. The teachings of the Italian school were introduced by Salomon de la Broue and Antoine de Pluvinel in the 16th century, but academic riding flourished in the 18th century at the schools of Versailles, Vienna, the Tuilieres and Saint Germain. The cadre noir consisted of civilians and military who comprised the teaching staff at the national riding school. A refined combination of tradition and modernity, age-old rules of the art of riding and modern technical developments generate a truly impressive performance. Horses and black-uniformed riders perform gracefully under a play of lights and shadows: the stylized Sauts d'Ecole are performed by thoroughbreds trained to dance to live classical music.

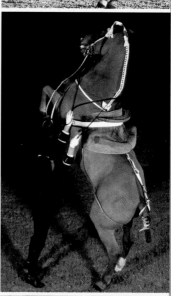

Right, National Riding School, four "Sauts d'Ecole". Below, the Horse Museum: the Riding School of Saumur in an engraving by Victor Adam.

On April 15, 1589, Duplessis-Mornay entered Saumur and installed his garrison. The next day the King of Navarre in turn entered the city, extremely satisfied to have taken over this key site on the Loire. A man of war and a shrewd diplomat, Duplessis-Mornay was also a learned theologian. In 1593 he founded a Protestant Academy in Saumur which was to bring fame to the city for almost a hundred years. Governor of Saumur for 32 years, he was a faithful servant of the Crown under two kings. Despite this, in 1621 he fell into disgrace and Louis XIII replaced him with a Catholic governor.

The political and military role of the castle thus came to an end. From then on, it began a less glorious epoch. For almost two centuries the old fortress, whose buildings were abandoned and gradually fell into ruin, was used as a gilded prison for various harebrained individuals or gentlemen of rank who had been imprisoned by the king. Their treatment was anything but harsh.

In 1768 the Marquis de Sade lived at the castle for a fortnight before being imprisoned at Pierre-Encise (near Lyon). Admiral de Kerguélen-Trémarec, explorer of the Indian Ocean, served four years imprisonment here (1774-1778) after he had returned from an unlucky expedition condemned for having abandoned a ship at sea. In 1779, during the American War of Independence, 800 English prisoners were enclosed in the manor as well as in the chapel of the building on the square and in other "annexes" on the bastions. Most of these were sailors as can be gathered from the graffiti they left, in which their names and the date of their capture are often accompanied by the image of a ship. New works of restoration began in 1811 and ended in 1814. This is undoubtedly when the galleries in the northeast wing were divided up into cells, since the engineer in charge of the works had been told to keep in mind the fact that "in a prison it is necessary to have the greatest possible number of isolated rooms, leaving only a few in common for those persons who were not lucky enough to have a room all to themselves".

The prison had just begun to function well when the provisory government ordered all the prisoners to be freed. In 1889 its status as a military building changed and a few years later it became a historical monument. Up until the end of the 19th century, Dr. Peton, mayor of Saumur, had thought of transforming it into a museum. His dream became reality in 1906 when the city bought the château from the State for the incredibly low sum of 2,500 francs and decided to begin restoration, sharing the costs with the Fine Arts Administration. Large carved windows, the remains of great fireplaces, the stained-glass windows of the chapel, and glazed tiles under the earth fills were all brought to light.

In particular, a coin with the effigy of Louis XIV provided an approximate date for the castle's transformation into a prison. In 1912 the first floor of the northeast wing, as well as the two towers which flank it, were allotted to the **Municipal Museum**, while the second floor is dedicated to the recently created **Horse Museum.**

BAUGÉ

The charming town of Baugé was founded at the beginning of the 11th century by Fulk Nera and four hundred years later it became one the favourite places visited by Yolanda of Aragon and her son, René of Anjou, titular King of Naples. Cousin and brother-in-law of Charles VIII, King of France, René was an extremely well educated prince, loved for his valour and gentle nature, which led to him being called "The Good". In 1455, he began to supervise personally the building work on the château of Baugé: with the simple and essential but elegant linearity of its shapes, it is charming and particularly light, thanks to the many windows on all sides. René of Anjou often stayed in this pleasant residence, located near woods rich in game and ideal for hunting, and the decorations in the various rooms on the first floor, reached by an elegant staircase, still recall him, with the coat of arms of the Sicilian Anjou family alternating with stars, angels and symbols of Christ's Cross. Indeed, in the chapel of a nearby hospice, a relic of the True Cross, known as the "Cross of Anjou", is venerated. The château, the right wing of which also contains an interesting oratory, today hosts a large **museum** with collections of precious examples of weapons, armour and ancient coins.

The elegant and simple Baugé château.

LE LUDE

The first castle to be built here, known at the time as Castellum Lusdi, was of wood as was customary in the Middle Ages. It was part of the property of the Counts of Anjou and was rebuilt in stone at the time of Fulk Nerra. A legend narrates that this was when the Loire was canalized and its course was deviated several kilometres to bring it closer to the castle, while the old river bed became a brook. Another legend of the same period refers to the fact that in the 10th century a demon inhabited the castle. In the guise of a servant he attempted to kill the owner. It was necessary to call in a bishop, Breviliguet, who used exorcisms to get rid of Satan's emissary.

Remodelling in the 13th century gave the fort a keep with walls, six towers and a deep moat. All that is left today of these structures is a subterranean vaulted room.

This defensive outpost on the Loire was acquired by the Vendôme family in 1378, but they abandoned it in the face of the relentless pursuit of the English troops under the Count of Warwick. In 1427 the stronghold was reconquered by Amboise de Loré and Gilles de Rais. Despite the fact that he was a Marshal of France, the latter was unable to escape the gallows after having been condemned for satanic rites.

The new owner from 1477 on, Jean II Daillon, sided with the faction that opposed the French dauphin. After Louis XI became king he pursued Jean for a long time and forced him to hide for seven years in a cave. Reconciled with the king, Daillon obtained important offices in court and was able to turn his attentions to transforming the castle into a building with three arms around a central court of honour. The work of renovation was completed by Jean II's two successors, both of whom were valorous soldiers. Louis XII's wing, Francis I's wing and the gardens laid out on the area of the old moat were thus added to Le Lude. Other transformations took place in the following centuries, such as the addition of a monumental façade towards the Loire, in Louis XVI style.

Below, a view of the château, and, right, the study with Italian style murals.

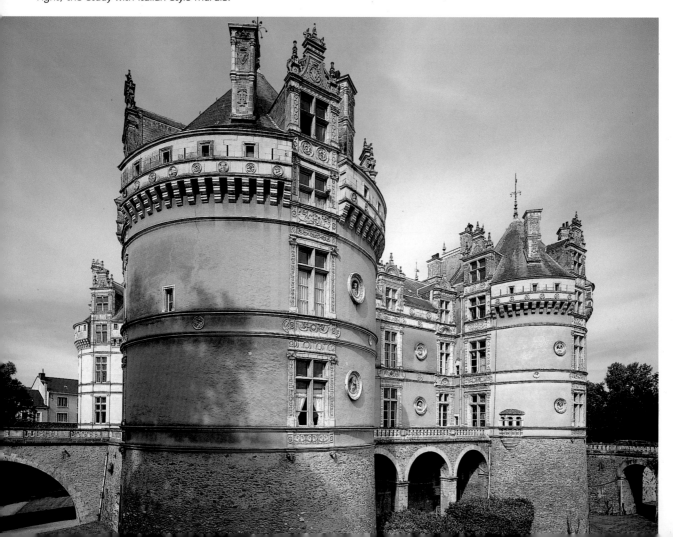

BRISSAC

Once upon a time numerous windmills stood in the Brissac area, close to Angers. During the Carolingian period a local miller who used to rob wheat by making holes in his clients' sacks was given the nickname of Brêche-Sac, which was later transformed into the present day name of Brissac. Fulk Nerra, the Count of Anjou, built a medieval castle as a military stronghold on the site and until 1434 the various owners were all warriors. The castle was then bought by Pierre de Brézé, an important figure in the royal court who was a minister both under Charles VII and under Louis XI, and who had the building modified. All that remains of this period are the two cylindrical corner towers of clearly

The wines of Brissac

Building of the vast castle of Brissac did not however distract attention from the foremost occupation of the surrounding area — cultivation of vines which have for centuries produced excellent results from the vineyards of the property.

Still today indeed, the castle of Brissac has some 28 hectares planted with vines extending around the manor, with grapes that produce three wines: two reds, one aged for a year and suited to accompanying red meats and game, the other lighter and more fruity, (suited to white meats) and a rosé (light and fruity, perfect with desserts or as an aperitif).

These are classified as Appellation Controllé and are produced under the historic label of "Château de Brissac". In addition, there will soon be a new AC for a white wine produced from a new vine planted in 2002 on a hill in the park overlooking the river Aubance. Known as the "Vigne des Cinq Siècles" it is produced to celebrate the Cossé Brissac family's five centuries of residence at the château.

Gothic style. In 1502 (some say 1492) René de Cossé acquired the castle and the surrounding land. Rumour has it that Jacques de Brézé suddenly sold it as the result of the double assassination of his wife Charlotte and her lover, for which he himself was to blame. According to certain legends, the châtelaine's ghost still haunts the castle. The religious wars had in part damaged the dwelling and it was finally transformed in 1614 by Charles II de Cossé, who held the office of Marshal of France. He turned to the well-known architect Jacques Corbineau, who designed an ambitious building for his patron. As planned, it would

have been unique for its time, with seven or eight floors, unusually high for buildings at the beginning of the 17th century.

Work was carried out on the central part of the old building, the towers of which were saved, until 1621. This was when death overtook Charles II, who had adhered to the Catholic League and as a faithful follower of Henry IV had opened the gates of Paris to him. The work came to a halt and the castle remained lower than planned and was roofed at this lower level. The influence of Italian Renaissance art, which had already made itself felt in other castles in the region of the Loire, is also clearly vis-

and with richly painted beams and cross-beams on the ceilings, still contain a great quantity of antique furniture and decorations. The Judith's Room mentioned above contains fine polychrome tapestries and an elegant mantlepiece; the large guardroom is decorated with other tapestries as well as with military curios such as saddles and suits of armour. The dining-room has a monumental staircase with two converging flights of stairs in Louis XIII style.

The various rooms also contain many paintings by well known painters which portray the members of the family.

Left, the "bedroom of the hunt" with tapestries from Tournai (16th-cent.), and, below, the bedroom of King Louis XIII, known as "Judith's Room", where on 12 August 1620 the king was reconciled with his mother, Maria de' Medici.

ible here. The façades, which face the town of Brissac on one side and the park around Aubance on the other, are oriented to the east and to the north, and even though they are elegant, they lack symmetry.

Tall chimneys abound on the steep slate roofs while the windows on the façades are surmounted by triangular or arched pediments, both complete and broken.

It was here that on 12 August 1620, Louis XIII was reconciled with his mother Marie de' Medici, Henry IV's widow, and for the occasion the Duc de Cossé organized great celebrations. The reconciliation, in the presence of representatives of the French clergy, took place in "Judith's Room" after the rebel troops had been driven from Ponts-de-Cé. In the following centuries the castle continued to belong to the Cossé family, which vaunted one of the most illustrious traditions of nobility in France.

The family includes four marshals, a grand master of the artillery, five governors of Paris and many other men of state. The apartments of the castle, lined with sculpted decoration

The Gothic tower on the south side, part of "a new castle half built on an old castle and half destroyed" (as the Duc de Cossé said regarding his residence) contains a private chapel with a marble bas-relief by David d'Angers, a local sculptor who worked in the first half of the 19th century.

Left, the private theatre that was decorated at the end of the 19th century.

Below, the château's kitchen.

SERRANT

In the 14th century the estate of Serrant belonged to the Le Brie family, but the building that existed at the time was only later transformed into the castle we see today. Louis XI granted Pontus Le Brie permission to create a stronghold on this spot, furnished with all kinds of defensive works.

Work began in 1546, under Charles Le Brie, who called in the famous architect Philibert Delorme, the designer of the wing of Chenonceau so daringly suspended over the Cher.

Extremely symmetrical and stylistically unified, despite the fact that the construction work continued throughout the 16th and 17th centuries, the castle of Serrant clearly displays the influence of Renaissance art, like all the luxurious châteaux of the Loire from the time of Francis I on.

The new Renaissance models (wide windows, pilasters, pediments, innovations of great elegance such as the domed roofs of the corner towers) harmonize perfectly with various archaic aspects (the corner towers, the symmetrical layout, the presence of deep moats filled with water).

This is all quite evident in the magnificent façade. Note should be made first of all of the sense of colour displayed in the use of shale and tufa, which create an elegant medley of brown and beige under the light line of the dormer windows and the dark slate roof. The double entrance is surmounted by a central body with windows and pilasters, on top of which is a sort of edicule with a triangular pediment. At the sides, rows of windows let light into the rooms of the castle, now conceived in terms of comfort and beauty. On the top floor the powerful corner towers are completely surrounded by a long balcony. They are roofed by two curious helmet-shaped domes which attempt to develop the older method of conical roofing. The upper hemisphere of each dome is surmounted by a lantern with a smaller, analogous, hemispherical roof. Stone bridges with arches supported by pilasters which terminate in pyramids lead over the wide moat at the side into the internal court.

While these structures were being built, the owners of the castle – after the Le Brie family – were the Duke of Montbazon Hercule de Rohan (around 1596) and then from 1636 on, the future Count of Serrant, Guillaume de Beutru. A member of the parliament of Rouen when he was only 22, he was then intendent for Touraine and selector of the king's ambassadors and court counsellor. He is remembered for his polished wit, his salacious sense of satire and as a member of the Academie Française as well as for his activities as a diplomat and ambassador. One of his heirs was his granddaughter Margaret, whose husband, Marquis of Vaubrun and lieutenant general of the King's army, fell in the battle of Altenheim in 1675. In memory of her consort, Margaret had the chapel built on the extension of the right wing, on which Jules Hardouin-Mansart, who had already created the Gallery of Mirrors in the castle of Versailles, worked. A monumental tomb for the marquis was built inside, executed

The room prepared for Napoleon in 1808 with the bust of the empress Marie Louise by Canova on the mantelpiece.

Facing page, above, the library, and, centre, the dining room decorated with huge Flemish tapestries.

by the sculptor Coysevox to a design attributed to Charles Le Brun.

Thereafter the castle of Serrant belonged to an Irish nobleman, Antoine Walsh, and, after 1830, to the Duke of Trémoïlle, to whose descendants it still belongs. Inside the château are magnificent furnishings, including tapestries of Brussels manufacture in the library (with thousands of books) and two busts by Antonio Canova of the Empress Marie Louise. Also worthy of note are the interior staircase, the dining-room and the ground floor ceilings, decorated with coffering. The chapel contains a polychrome relief with a *Pietà* in addition to the mausoleum of the Marquis of Vaubrun.

MONTGEOFFROY

Lying 24 km to the east of Angers this chateau was built in the 18th century by the Marquis de Contades, marshall of France under Louis XV, on the site of an earlier residence acquired by his family a century earlier. Two 15th-century towers of the older castle still exist on either side of the façade of this attractive chateau. The interior is decorated with original furniture belonging to the De Contades family who still maintain the property of Montgeoffroy.

An interesting view of the castle.

The variegated structure of the castle of Plessis-Bourré is still perfectly intact and magnificently furnished in keeping with the 15th-century appearance. In 1911 it was enhanced and attentively restored by the new owner, Senator Vaisse, an ancestor of the present owners. Its structure and appearance have earned it recognition as a historic monument (1931) and, open to the public since 1955, it offers a spectacular and dramatic setting that is historically authentic.

It has obviously, therefore, often been chosen as the perfect location for many famous films, such as "Peau d'Âne" by Jacques Demy, "Le Bossu" by Philippe de Broca, and "Fanfan la Tulipe" by Gérard Krawczyk.

PLESSIS-BOURRÉ

Around twenty kilometres from Angers, surrounded by a large, deep moat making it appear to rest on a small island, the château of Plessis-Bourré, completely white under the shining slate roof, appears in all its Renaissance splendour which has remained perfectly intact throughout the centuries. Jean Bourré was Secretary of Finance and the Treasurer of France under Louis XI. A man of many interests, and intrigued by alchemy, Jean Bourré's creative spirit found its fulfilment in the building of many spectacular châteaux (Langeais, Jazzé, Vaulx). In 1462, he purchased the Plessis-le-Vent estates and six years later began work on his new château, the only one he built which has completely preserved its original features and which is, without doubt, one of the most beautiful and imposing of all the châteaux along the Loire. Completed in four years, the external structure looks like a fortress, with its rectangular perimeter emphasized at the corners by four towers (the tallest of which, the donjon, is 44 metres high), designed to remain outside the shooting range of any enemy guns, but also impregnable to direct assault, with moving stairways and towers, thanks to its high walls which are over 2 metres thick. A 43-metre bridge crosses the moat and leads to a double drawbridge and the original 3-metre wide platform – an element almost exclusive to this château – which runs around the château and was used for positioning artillery. However, we have only to pass through the huge entrance gate and enter the vast internal courtyard (a surface area of 1360 sq.m.) to discover, behind the rough, fortified appearance, a splendid elegant Renaissance residence, still entirely furnished and decorated according to the wishes of Jean Bourré's wife, Marguerite de Feschal, five centuries ago. Corridors with low arched vaults, stairways and galleries follow on from each other leading to a charming series of halls and rooms which had the honour of welcoming first Louis XI, in 1473, and then Charles VIII, in 1487.

In the huge Louis XVI hall the 18th-century furniture blends well with the d'Aubusson tapestries and the floral motifs realized as ornaments for the doors by the great cabinet-maker David d'Angers. In the Louis XV hall the walls are covered in elegant panels with floral motifs, while the great hall is incredibly light and airy, yet warmed by splendid boiseries, and lastly the Parliament hall served as an imposing dining-room, with its monumental richly decorated fireplace and Flanders tapestries. On the first floor is the Guardroom, noted for its stupendous ceiling, unique of its kind, which offers one of the most beautiful examples of 15th-century art; of painted wood, it is divided into six large sections which are, in turn, composed of four hexagons which develop around a central rhombus. A total, therefore, of twenty-four large pictures painted on a blue-green background depicting famous proverbs, allegorical figures, protagonists of French legends, humorous scenes, all reflecting the most classical alchemic symbolism, to which all the statues adorning the room also clearly refer. Worthy of note again is the master bedroom, with its splendid and austere Renaissance furnishings; the library where over three thousand books are kept along a 36 metre gallery; and the chapel of Ste-Anne, containing interesting examples of sacred art. This grand residential complex is equipped to this day with the old, well preserved service rooms, cellars in particular, and the attics located on the top floor, which have magnificent chestnut-wood trussed roofing, and from where the patrol passage around the roof is reached.

Left, a general view of this majestic castle.

Right, from top, the splendidly furnished Louis XV room and the library.

Below, the beautiful statue of the Athanor, alchemic emblem of the philosophical cauldron.

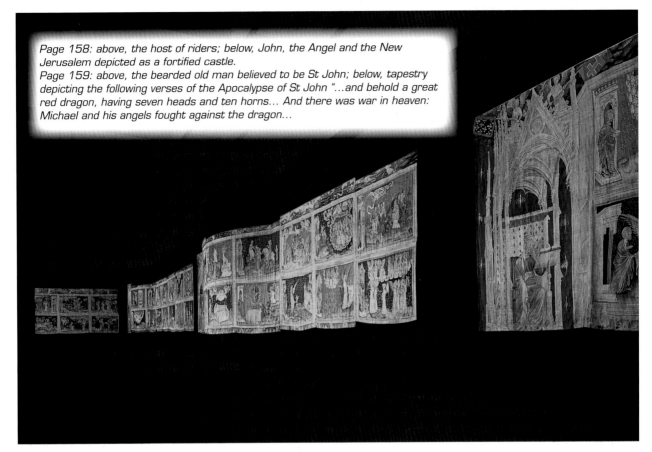

Page 158: above, the host of riders; below, John, the Angel and the New Jerusalem depicted as a fortified castle.
Page 159: above, the bearded old man believed to be St John; below, tapestry depicting the following verses of the Apocalypse of St John "...and behold a great red dragon, having seven heads and ten horns... And there was war in heaven: Michael and his angels fought against the dragon...

The mighty round towers of the château of Angers.   *The gallery with the famous "Apocalypse Tapestries."*

ANGERS

Situated on the shores of the Maine river, Angers was once inhabited by fierce Celtic peoples who tenaciously opposed Roman penetration.

After the period of the Norman invasions (9th century) Fulk Nera, Count of Anjou, had a castle built here. This first stronghold was replaced by a better furnished architectural complex built by Louis IX, known as Saint Louis, between 1228 and 1238, which was then further enlarged by Louis I and Louis II of Anjou, who had the Gothic chapel built.

The court of René of Anjou, known as the Good, regent of Sicily and Jerusalem, resided here. A man of letters and benefactor of the local community, he was fond of fêtes and tournaments which were often held at the castle. In an illuminated manuscript which he himself executed, René illustrated in words and images the pomp that accompanied the tournaments in the castle of Angers.

The Wars of Religion later led to the decline of the castle.

The series of **Apocalypse Tapestries**, commissioned by Louis I in 1373, is now on exhibit inside the castle. This magnificent textile, originally 140 metres long, is based on cartoons by the painter Hennequin de Bruges, and was woven by Nicolas Bataille. This long series of panels which illustrate the "Book of Revelations" of St John was in the archbishopric of Arles in 1400 and after 1474 in the church of St-Maurice in Angers. In 1782 the tapestries disappeared, to be recovered in 1848 by a canon, Joubert, who had them restored. Each panel is accompanied by the figure of St John, who participates in and illustrates the scene. The original captions were removed during the 19th-century restoration because of their poor state of preservation.

John's story is difficult to understand and full of allegories whose meaning is not always clear. In the tapestries this occult meaning is respected. In the still extant panels the story begins with John, upon divine invitation, describing his visions for the good of the seven churches, shown as chapels. The symbolism present in this scene pervades the entire work, as is noted in the following panels in which John sees the Messiah, with specific attributes, amidst figures which allegorically represent the accomplishments of Creation. After a scene of homage to the Messiah comes the lamentation of the saint and the beginning of the revelation of the divine secrets after the adoration of the sacred lamb.

The four riders of the Apocalypse, on different coloured horses, are revealed and after them comes the salvation of the souls of the dead in the service of God. After the identification of the chosen people, new secrets are revealed in the presence of God and an angel. The forces of nature demonstrate their might, unleashed by the first four peals of the divine trumpets

in the panels representing the storm, the star of fire and the eagle. At the fifth and sixth peals, the disorder in the universe increases. In the panels that follow, the mysterious words of the seven claps of thunder are revealed to St John and he symbolically devours the book of the angel. After John's appraisal of celestial harmony come four panels which narrate the adventure of the two witnesses saved by God and the announcement of the imminent arrival of the Messiah and the Last Judgment. This is followed by the chapter in which Satan, in different forms, persecutes Creation, first as a dragon, attacking a pregnant woman who is defended by St Michael and battling with the faithful, then as an idolatrous marine monster, and finally as a land monster. After these scenes, angels announce the New Testament, the fall of Babylon and the sufferings of the damned. Then, after the just have been saved they are received by God, while the infidels face divine wrath (which symbolically reaps them like grapes at harvest time). The representation of the seven scourges which accompany the wrath of God is followed by the appearance of three satanic beasts and the whore of Babylon, mother of abominations; they all finally fall, together with the three beasts and Satan himself. The series of tapestries ends with the image of the celestial Jerusalem, of which St John measures the perfection and finally prostrates himself before the Trinity.

INDEX